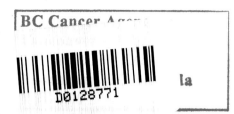
Using This Book Is Simple

This book is designed for busy people. It is mainly graphic;
the drawings convey much of the information. Text is minimal.

HOW TO STRETCH

First read pages 4 to 7 for the basics on stretching.

GO BY THE FEEL

Next follow through the series of six stretches on pages 10 to 13. This
will teach you how to stretch.

STRETCHING ROUTINES

Skip ahead now and take a look at the routines on pages 19 to 39. They
are the heart of the book.

STRETCHING INSTRUCTIONS

Read the instructions for each of the stretches *(pp. 65 to 84)* the first
time you do them. (See the page reference under each stretch in the
routines.)

Then select a program and

S–T–R–E–T–C–H

IF YOU ENJOYED THE BOOK, TRY THE SOFTWARE.

StretchWare is a computer program developed from the stretching
routines outlined in this book. The User Manual for StretchWare is
included in the appendix of this book, along with ordering information.
Read the book, use the software, and

S–T–R–E–T–C–H

STRETCHING
IN THE OFFICE

Bob Anderson

Illustrated by Jean Anderson

Distributed in the United States by Publishers Group West and in Canada by Publishers Group Canada.

Library of Congress Cataloging-in-Publication Data
Anderson, Bob, 1945–
   Stretching in the Office / Bob Anderson; illustrated by Jean Anderson
      p.   cm.
   Includes bibliographical references and index.
   ISBN 0-936070-29-3
   1. Stretching exercises.   2. Clerks—Health and hygiene.
3. Electronic data processing personnel—Health and hygiene.   I. Title.
RA781.63 .A533 2002
613.7'1—dc21   2002006918

We are grateful to Fellowes Computerware, Itasca, Illinois, for permission to reprint the drawing "Ergoman" on page 46.

7 6 5 4 3 2 1—08 07 06 05 04 03 02
(Lowest numbers indicate number and year of this printing)

Printed in the U.S.A.

PLEASE NOTE: The stretches, exercises, and other information in this book are not meant to substitute for medical diagnosis and/or treatment. If you have any physical problems or health conditions, please consult with your physician or health professional before trying any new physical activity.

Write, call, or email us for a free copy of our catalog:
Shelter Publications, Inc.
P. O. Box 279
Bolinas, CA 94924
415-868-0280
E-mail: shelter@shelterpub.com

Visit Our Website
SHELTER ONLINE
www.shelterpub.com

Other than the invention of the steam engine by Watt and the subsequent mechanization and industrialization of human work, perhaps no single technological advancement in how work is organized and performed has caused as much concern among humans, and their social and technical organizations, as the invention and subsequent proliferation of the computer.

Harry L. Davis, in foreword to
Ergonomics in Computerized Offices
Etienne Grandjean

Stretching

in the Office

Contents

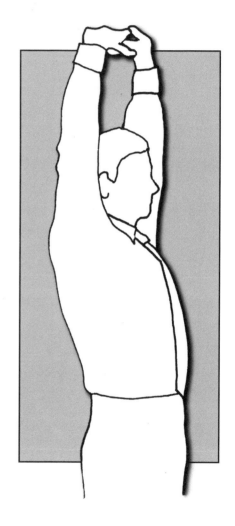

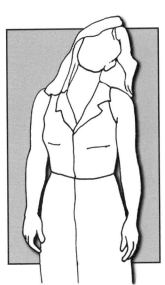

Introduction

A funny thing happened on the way to the electronic revolution. Large numbers of us ended up sitting at desks, working at computers. And that, as so many people have discovered, has its problems, its downsides.

Repetitive strain injuries (such as carpal tunnel syndrome and tendinitis) of the wrists, hands, and arms have risen by 80% since 1990, according to the U. S. Bureau of Labor Statistics, and are now the single largest category of workplace-related injuries. In fact, they are now being described as the workplace epidemic of the nineties.

Neck and shoulder stiffness, lower back pain, stiff muscles, and tight joints are all common among people working at computers. All of these conditions are the body signaling that something is wrong.

The human body was not designed for long periods of sitting. Holding still for hours at a time is a relatively recent phenomenon in human history. For some two million years, our ancestors had to use their bodies and muscles daily. In nomadic times activity was required for hunting and gathering. With the agricultural revolution, tilling the soil, planting, and harvesting required physical effort. After the industrial revolution and the advent of machines and motor vehicles, however, physical activity began to decline; nevertheless millions still worked in factories and assembly lines, using their bodies daily.

Now all that is changing — fast. The electronic revolution has meant that increasing numbers of people must spend more and more time sitting very still, working with computers, and the resultant problems are multiplying.

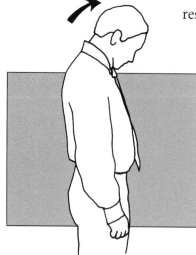

This book is for people who work at a computer and/or a desk and want to do something to counteract the negative effects that fixed positions and sedentary office work have on their bodies.

Stretching is a wonderful solution. It is a very simple activity that can make you feel better. It is gentle, peaceful, and relaxing. If practiced correctly, it can prevent many computer-related problems before they start and—if an injury has occurred—can help with rehabilitation.

Stretching can be done almost anywhere and at any time. It requires no special equipment, no special clothes, no special skills. You can stretch periodically throughout the day wherever you are. It can often be done while you are doing something else: when you're at an office meeting, while on the phone, or while you're waiting for the computer to process information.

Bob Anderson has taught stretching to people for almost 30 years and has seen gratifying results from this simplest of all physical activities — for people in all walks of life, from ordinary citizens to people in wheelchairs to world-class athletes.

This book applies the basic principles of stretching to the problems inherent in working at a computer and sitting still for long periods of time. It will show you how taking short stretching breaks throughout the day can make you feel better, prevent injuries, and lead to a more productive workday.

But first, let's take a closer look at typical problems of the computer workplace.

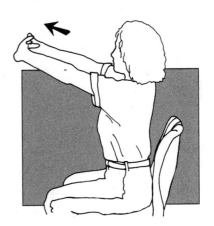

Computer & Desk Problems

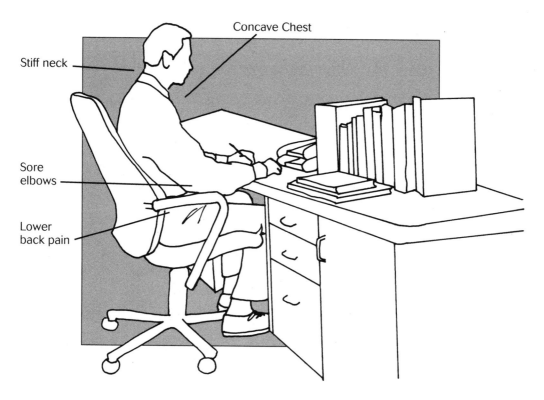

Concave Chest

Stiff neck

Sore elbows

Lower back pain

A typical desk setup

- **Back pain** When you sit for long periods, your spine tends to compress. If your posture is bad, gravity accentuates the problem, which can lead to back pain.

- **Stiff muscles** Not moving for long periods of time can cause neck and shoulder pain.

- **Tight joints** Inactivity can cause joints to tighten, which makes moving more difficult or even painful.

- **Poor circulation** When you sit very still, blood tends to settle in the lower legs and feet and does not circulate easily throughout the body.

- **Repetitive strain injuries** These injuries are caused by repetitive movement, often of the hands. For example, carpal tunnel syndrome, a type of wrist pain, can result from improper use of the hands and/ or poor positioning at the workstation.

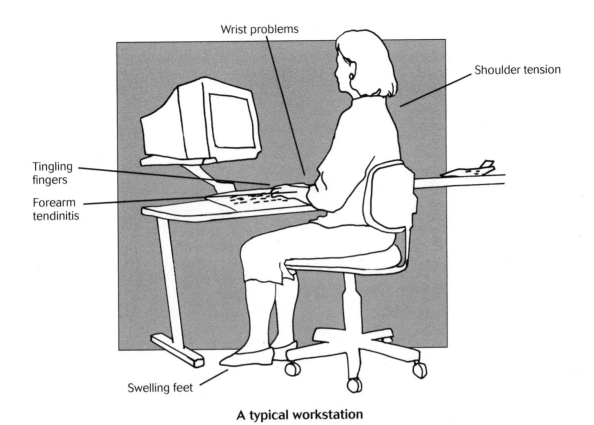

A typical workstation

• **Tension and stress** Intense mental focus can produce physical tension (stiffness and pain), which can lead to mental stress—a debilitating cycle. Facial tension and a tight jaw can cause headaches.

Many of these problems can be solved by ergonomics—the science involved with proper type and positioning of office equipment in relation to the body (*see pp. 46 to 50*). However, no matter how sound the ergonomics, your body still suffers from long periods of sitting and inactivity. What can you do throughout the long work day to help prevent these problems?

You can stretch!

When to Stretch

Stretching every hour or so throughout the day can help you avoid stiffness and muscle soreness, and make you feel better. You can stretch:

- On the job, to release nervous tension
- While your computer is processing something, if only for 5 to 10 seconds
- Whenever you feel stiff, sore, or tired
- Before and after taking a walk
- In the morning, just after getting up, and in the evening, before sleep
- When you need more energy
- Whenever you want to focus and do your best

Where to Stretch

You can stretch at your computer, or at your desk, and in a variety of other places. Here's a chance to be creative. For example, you can stretch:

- When you're a passenger in a car, or in a bus, or train on the way to work
- At your desk
- While on the phone
- At the copy machine
- At the filing cabinet or drinking fountain
- At office meetings
- While standing or waiting in line
- Before getting up to go anywhere

Benefits of Stretching

Stretching is just about the simplest of all physical activities. It is the perfect antidote for long periods of inactivity and holding still. Regular stretching throughout the day will:

- Reduce muscle tension
- Improve circulation
- Reduce anxiety, stress, and fatigue
- Improve mental alertness
- Decrease the risk of injury
- Make your work easier
- Tune your mind into your body
- Make you feel better!

IF YOU ARE INJURED

Please note: If you have an injury or any type of recurring soreness as described on pages 2 and 3, see a doctor or health care provider now. These stretches are not intended to cure serious problems. If you have the symptoms of a repetitive strain injury, some damage has already been done. If you do not take the right steps, damage could be permanent. For more details, see the section on repetitive strain injuries starting on page 44.

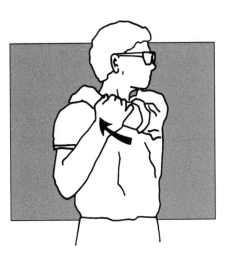

How to Stretch

THE RIGHT WAY TO STRETCH

- Breathe easily
- Relax
- Tune into your body
- Focus on muscles and joints being stretched
- *Feel* the stretch
- Be guided by the *feel* of the stretch
- No bouncing!
- No pain!

THE WRONG WAY TO STRETCH

- Holding your breath
- Being in a hurry
- Not being focused on your body
- Stretching while tense
- Bouncing
- Stretching to the point of pain

TWO PHASES

There are two phases to each stretch: the easy stretch and the developmental stretch. They are done one after the other.

THE EASY STRETCH

Stretch until you feel a slight mild tension and hold for 5–10 seconds. *Relax.* As you hold the stretch, the feeling of tension should diminish. If it doesn't, ease off slightly into a more comfortable stretch. The easy stretch maintains flexibility, loosens muscles and tight tendons, and reduces muscle tension.

THE DEVELOPMENTAL STRETCH

Now, move a fraction of an inch farther into the stretch until you feel mild tension again. Hold for 5 to 10 seconds. Again, the feeling should diminish or stay the same. If the tension increases or becomes painful, you are overstretching —back off into a more comfortable stretch. The developmental stretch further reduces tension and increases flexibility.

KEEP THE FOLLOWING POINTS IN MIND

- Always stretch within your comfortable limits, never to the point of pain.

- Breathe slowly, rhythmically and under control. Do not hold your breath.

- Take your time. The long-sustained, mild stretch reduces unwanted muscle tension and tightness.

- Do not compare yourself with others. We are all different. Comparisons may lead to overstretching.

- If you are stretching correctly, the stretch feeling should slightly subside as you hold the stretch.

- Any stretch that grows in intensity or becomes painful means you are overstretching—the drastic stretch. *(See page 13.)*

PAY ATTENTION TO HOW EACH STRETCH FEELS

Hold only stretch tensions that feel good. Relax while you concentrate on the area being stretched.

IMPORTANT

No bouncing
No pain

HOW FAR SHOULD I STRETCH?

Your body is different every day. Be guided by how the stretch feels.

STRETCHING IS NOT EXERCISE!

You are stretching, not exercising. You don't need to push it. Stretching is a mild, gentle activity.

GIVE IT 2 TO 3 WEEKS FOR BENEFITS

The benefits come from regularity. Stick with it and see how you feel in a few weeks.

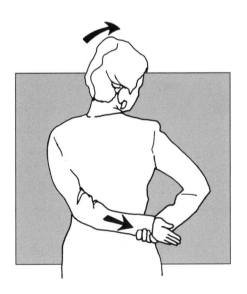

Watch a cat stretch. Cats are graceful and coordinated. They instinctively stretch to keep muscles tuned, joints flexible. Notice how the cat feels the stretch, tests the tension, relaxes, sometimes yawns, focuses on the stretch.

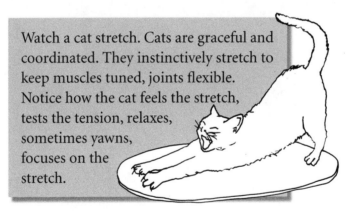

Go by the Feel

The Key to Safe & Effective Stretching

Here we will walk through a series of stretches that will help you understand the phrase "Go by the *feel* of the stretch." This is far more important than how *far* you stretch, or how far others stretch. This series of 6 stretches will take you 1 to 2 minutes.

Read pages 6 to 7 on how to stretch, so you understand the principles of what we are doing here.

The following stretches can be done either sitting or standing.

Note: *Shading indicates the areas being stretched.*

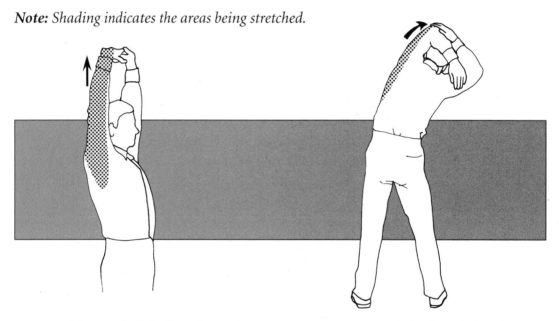

Start with knees slightly flexed. Interlace fingers over your head, reverse your hands (palms face up), and push your arms gently upward until you feel a mild stretch. Pay attention to how this feels. Don't overstretch. (You may not be able to stretch as far as shown above—don't worry about it.) Hold comfortably for 8 to 10 seconds. You should be able to say "I feel the stretch but it doesn't hurt."

Next, grasp your left elbow behind your head with your right hand until you feel a slight stretch. Then lean slightly to the right. Hold 8 to 10 seconds. Don't hold your breath; breathe easily. Then repeat for the other side: hold your right elbow with your left hand, stretch gently, and lean to the left. Don't stretch too far.

Now go back and repeat the first stretch. Knees slightly flexed, interlace fingers above head. Reverse hands and push arms gently upward. How does this *feel*? Is this stretch any easier now? Are you a little more flexible? If you do these stretches in front of a mirror, you can see how you look and also if you are stretching any farther as you go through this series.

Next raise your shoulders up toward your ear lobes with controlled tension. Hold 5–6 seconds, then relax shoulders downward. "Shoulders hang, shoulders down." Keep your jaw relaxed (your jaw should be relaxed in all the stretches).

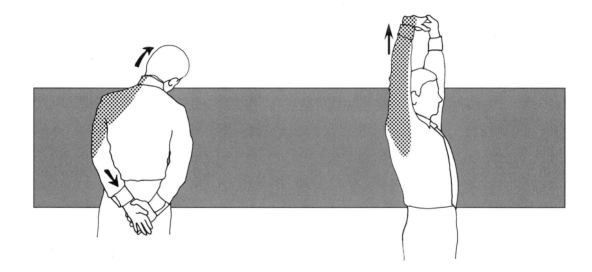

Now reach behind you and hold onto your left wrist with your right hand. Pull your right hand down and over to the right as you lean your head in the same direction. Hold 8 to 10 seconds. This stretches the neck, shoulders, and arms. Now switch and do the other side. Be sure you hold only stretches that are mild and comfortable.

Now go back and repeat the beginning stretch. With knees slightly flexed, interlace your fingers above your head. Reverse your hands and push your arms gently upward. Now how does it feel? Most people will feel more flexible in this stretch after going through this series. Again, a mirror may be helpful in showing you if you are gaining flexibility doing these stretches.

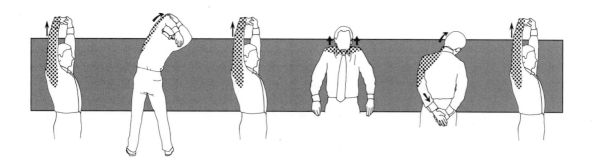

Above is a summary of the stretches we have just gone through. These are excellent to do any time at your computer to relieve neck and shoulder stiffness, to reduce stress, and to relax.

The purpose of this series of stretches has been to get you to focus on the areas being stretched, to *feel* the stretch.

Sometimes it's helpful to play with the mild tension created by the stretch. Go back and forth slowly and focus on how it feels. Go from the easy stretch into the developmental stretch *(see below)* and back again. Breathe easily, relax and concentrate on the areas being stretched.

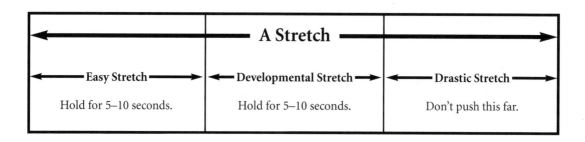

	A Stretch	
← Easy Stretch →	← Developmental Stretch →	← Drastic Stretch →
Hold for 5–10 seconds.	Hold for 5–10 seconds.	Don't push this far.

Once you learn this principle, once you actually feel what stretching is doing for your muscles and tendons, you will be able to apply the principle to any stretch.

You will have learned not to overstretch. You will have learned the most important principle of stretching, which is to *go by the feel.*

Keep On Stretchin'

To stay loose, stretch regularly throughout the day. Keep this book in your desk drawer, or open on your desk.

Stretching Routines

Stretching Routines

The routines that follow (*pp. 19 to 39*) are designed for easy visual reference. They are grouped by common situations, circumstances, or time of day. The important thing is to stretch regularly throughout the day.

Most of these programs take 1 to 2 minutes.

First, read the *general* stretching instructions on pages 6 to 7.

Then find the program that best suits your needs.

Lay the book open on your desk and follow the drawings.

Each time you do a stretch for the first time, read the *specific* instructions for that stretch on pages 64 to 84. (See the page reference under each stretch.) After you follow the instructions a few times, you'll know how to do each stretch correctly. From then on, simply look at the drawings.

You may want to photocopy some of these pages to keep in your desk or on the wall.

Alternative: Another way to get started is to turn to page 65 and do the stretches one by one, following the detailed instructions. This is a good way to get familiar with each stretch.

Note: *The shaded areas indicate the part of your body being stretched.*

Good Morning!

(Startup) Stretches

Here's a good way to start the day. While your computer is warming up, do these stretches to loosen up and get ready for work. Turn on your body while you're turning on your computer.

- Relax.
- Focus on the muscles being stretched.

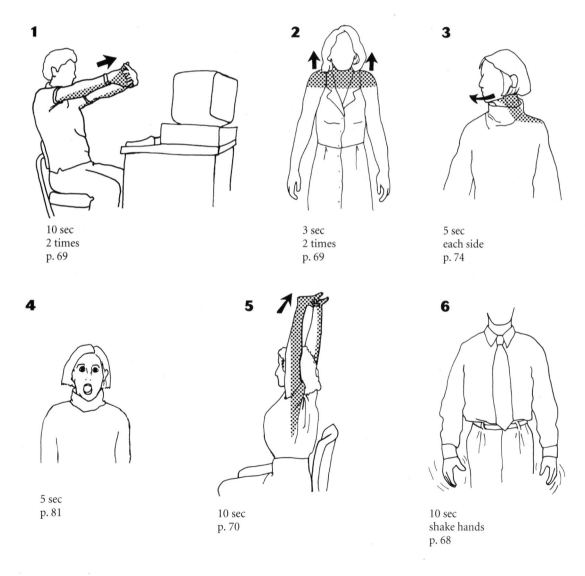

1

10 sec
2 times
p. 69

2

3 sec
2 times
p. 69

3

5 sec
each side
p. 74

4

5 sec
p. 81

5

10 sec
p. 70

6

10 sec
shake hands
p. 68

Neck & Shoulder Stiffness

Elapsed time: 1 minute

We all feel stiff from tension or holding still at the computer. Do these stretches any time of the day when you feel stiffness in the neck and/or shoulders. Each stretch takes 10 seconds or less and each one will help you relax.

- *Feel* each stretch
- Breathe easily

1

3 sec
2 times
p. 69

2

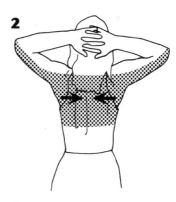

5 sec
p. 71

3

5 sec
each side
p. 73

4

10 sec
each side
p. 72

5

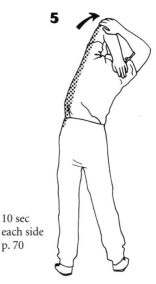

10 sec
each side
p. 70

Stretching in the Office ©2002 Robert A. Anderson, Jean E. Anderson & Shelter Publications, Inc.

70 seconds

Sitting for long periods is one of the biggest causes of lower back pain. Do these stretches throughout the day to move the lower back muscles and to get some circulation going. This is a good way to help avoid back problems.

Be sure to get up and move as often as possible throughout the day.

1

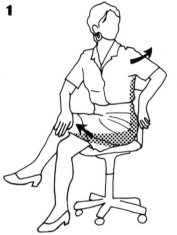

10 sec
each side
p. 80

2

10 sec
2 times
p. 75

3

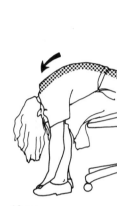

10 sec
p. 81

4

10 sec
each leg
p. 79

Caution: *If you have a history of lower back problems, consult a reliable physician who will give you tests to see exactly where the problem lies. Ask your physician which of the stretches shown in this book would be of most help to you. Also, check out the Back Revolution® on page 93; it has helped many people with back problems.*

Stretches for Keyboard Operators

Elapsed time: 76 seconds

Many people do not understand this, but working on a keyboard all day, day after day, is physically demanding. Repetitive strain injuries (RSIs) from mouse and keyboard use have risen dramatically. The routine below is specifically designed for keyboard operators and their potential (or actual) problems.

- If you are injured, see a doctor (preferably one with RSI experience) for advice on which stretches will help you recover.

- If you are not injured now, do these stretches throughout the day as preventive medicine. (Stretch while making "saves," for example.)

- *See the section, A Pain-Free Body, pp. 44 to 57, for more on RSI problems.*

1

8 sec
p. 67

2

8 sec
p. 67

3

10 sec
2 times
p. 69

4

10–15 sec
p. 70

5

10 sec
each arm
p. 70

6

10 sec
p. 81

> **Move**
> *It's important to move: take a 1-minute break every 10–15 minutes, or a 5-minute break every half hour; get up and move around.*

Stretching in the Office ©2002 Robert A. Anderson, Jean E. Anderson & Shelter Publications, Inc.

Stretches for Graphic Artists

80 seconds

Concentrated effort on visual images puts a strain on your body as well as your eyes. Using a stylus with a drawing tablet can cause finger and wrist problems. Take frequent breaks to do these stretches, or do them while you're waiting for the computer to process information.

- Look at the stretching index on pages 94 to 95 for some other ideas.
- You can also do some exercises or move around (*see pp. 58 to 61*).

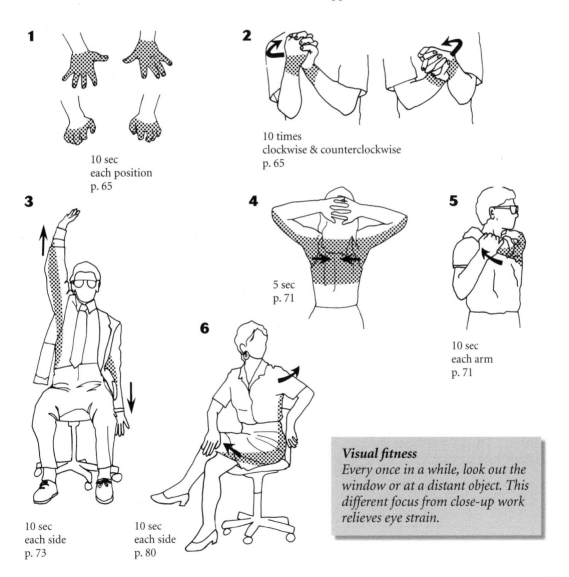

1

10 sec
each position
p. 65

2

10 times
clockwise & counterclockwise
p. 65

3

10 sec
each side
p. 73

4

5 sec
p. 71

5

10 sec
each arm
p. 71

6

10 sec
each side
p. 80

> **Visual fitness**
> *Every once in a while, look out the window or at a distant object. This different focus from close-up work relieves eye strain.*

Office Meeting Stretches

Everyone knows the physical by-products of meetings: drowsiness, stiffening, back and leg pain, etc. Try a few stretches during a meeting to counteract the effects of sitting.

See if you can educate other people in your meetings about the value of stretching. It isn't so weird!

- Do these in any order.
- Breathe deeply.
- Maintain good posture.
- Every so often, tighten your abdominal muscles, pull in your stomach and hold. Then relax.
- *See index of stretches on pages 94 to 95 for other ideas.*

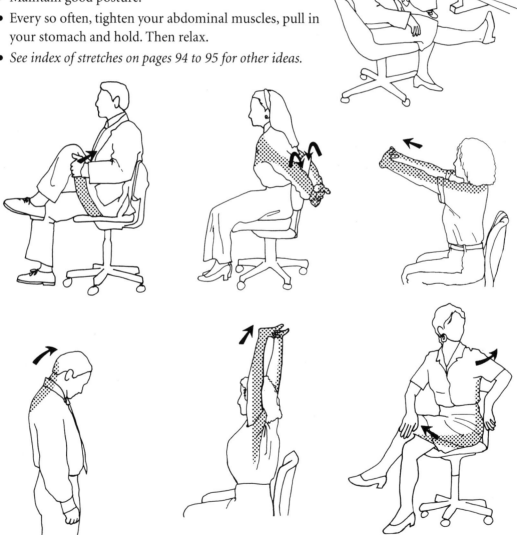

Stretching in the Office ©2002 Robert A. Anderson, Jean E. Anderson & Shelter Publications, Inc.

Online Stretches

1 minute

No matter how fast your modem, you're always waiting for something to load while online. (This will probably never change, for even as modems get faster and faster, files get larger and larger.) These stretches are for your upper body, especially neck, shoulders, and wrists.

- Whenever you are reading online, and not using the keyboard or mouse, you can do upper body stretches using both arms.

- After you follow this program a few times, you'll know these stretches by heart; thereafter do them frequently while online.

- Stretches 1–6 are a special routine. *See pages 10 to 13 for details.*

If there isn't time to do them all at one time, break the routine into short combinations: 1, 2, 3 or 4, 5, 6 or 7, 8.

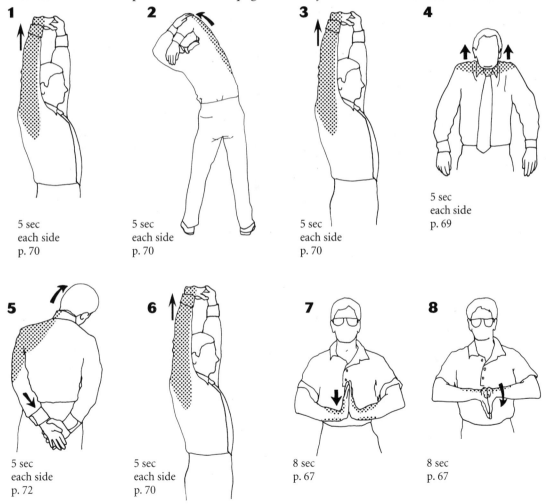

1
5 sec
each side
p. 70

2
5 sec
each side
p. 70

3
5 sec
each side
p. 70

4
5 sec
each side
p. 69

5
5 sec
each side
p. 72

6
5 sec
each side
p. 70

7
8 sec
p. 67

8
8 sec
p. 67

Stressed-Out Stretches

Elapsed time: 90 seconds

- Had a tough day?
- Computer giving you problems?
- Going to an important meeting?
- Need to relax?

There come those inevitable times during the day when the body signals it has had an overdose of stress. Don't let tension build up and ruin your good work. Pace yourself throughout the day. Take frequent stretch breaks!

- Breathe deeply.
- Take a few minutes to do these stretches.

1

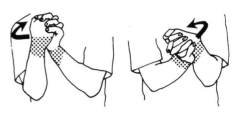

10 sec
each position
p. 65

2

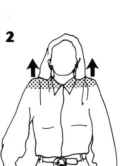

3 sec
2 times
p. 69

3

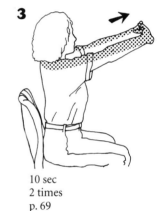

10 sec
2 times
p. 69

4

15 sec
each arm
p. 71

5

10 sec
p. 70

6

5 sec
each side
p. 73

Stretching in the Office ©2002 Robert A. Anderson, Jean E. Anderson & Shelter Publications, Inc.

Really Stressed-Out Stretches!

70 seconds

Still tense? Has it just been one of those days? In cases of advanced stress, do these stretches in addition to those on the opposite page.

- Take some more deep breaths.
- Sit quietly or meditate for a few minutes.
- Walking or any kind of movement or exercise relieves stress.
- Relax and take a few minutes for yourself!

1

5 sec
p. 81

2

5 sec
p. 71

3

10 sec
each side
p. 73

4

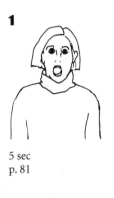

10 sec
p. 81

5

10 sec
2 times
p. 75

6

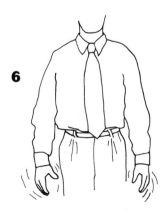

10 sec
shake hands
p. 68

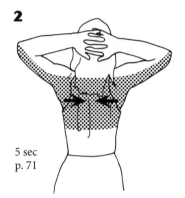

Spontaneous Stretches

(Do whenever you can)

The idea here is to take a stretching break whenever you have the chance—
to rejuvenate your body and recharge your energy. These stretches take
only a few seconds each.

- Do these in any order.
- Pay attention to your body and stretch the parts that need it most.
- Be creative and be relaxed.
- *See stretching index on pp. 94 to 95 for other ideas.*

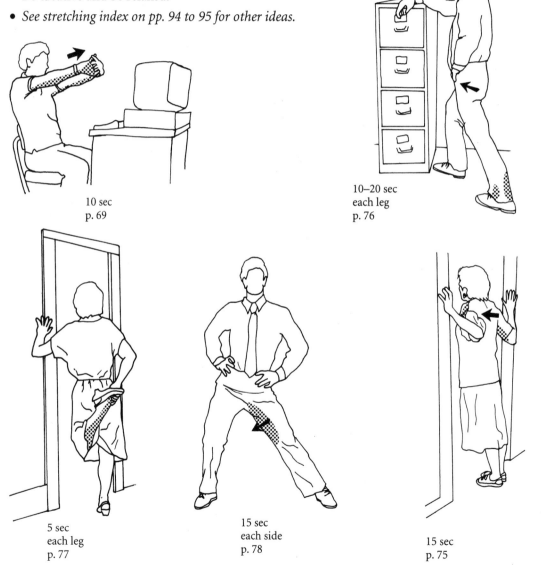

10 sec
p. 69

10–20 sec
each leg
p. 76

5 sec
each leg
p. 77

15 sec
each side
p. 78

15 sec
p. 75

Stretching in the Office ©2002 Robert A. Anderson, Jean E. Anderson & Shelter Publications, Inc.

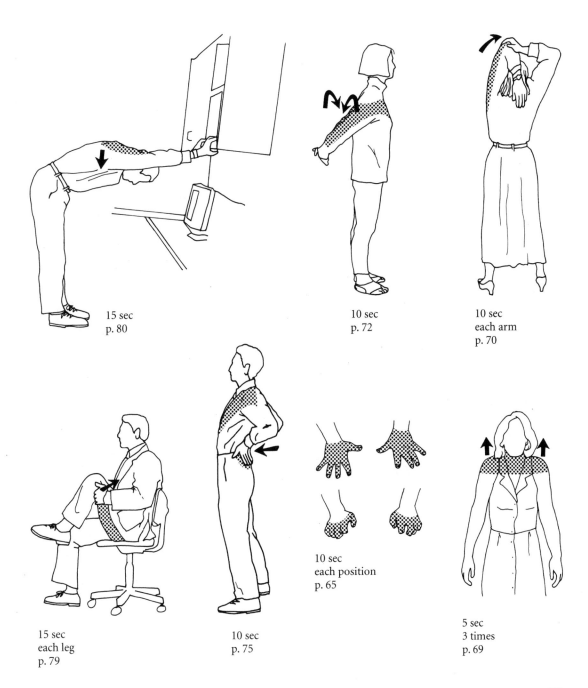

15 sec
p. 80

10 sec
p. 72

10 sec
each arm
p. 70

15 sec
each leg
p. 79

10 sec
p. 75

10 sec
each position
p. 65

5 sec
3 times
p. 69

Copy Machine Stretches

(or Waiting-for-the-Printer Stretches)

Here is a chance to stretch while you're waiting around. It's a bonus—it doesn't take any extra time!

- Stretch while you wait for the copies.
- Do any of the stretches in this book while making copies. Be inventive!
- Copy this page on the copy machine (!) and put it on the wall by the copy machine.

Who says you can't do two things at once!

Stretching in the Office ©2002 Robert A. Anderson, Jean E. Anderson & Shelter Publications, Inc.

On-the-Phone Stretches

How much time do you spend on the phone each day? All these can be done with a phone in hand. With a headset they are even easier.

- Make a copy of this page and keep it next to your phone.
- Look through the index of stretches *(pp. 94 to 95)* for ideas on other stretches to do while on the phone.

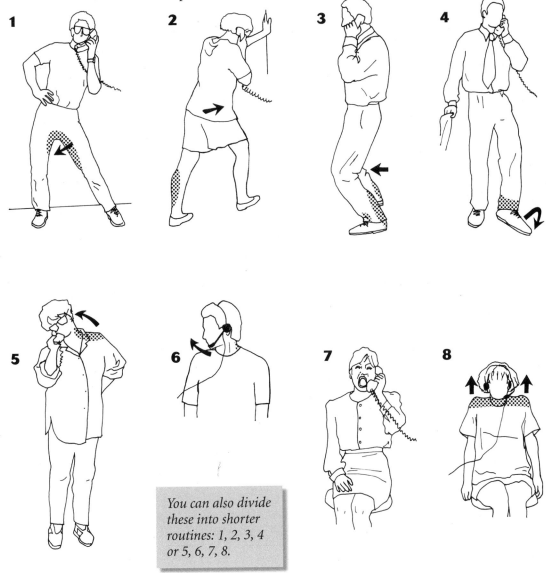

You can also divide these into shorter routines: 1, 2, 3, 4 or 5, 6, 7, 8.

Before-Walking Stretches

Elapsed time: 2 minutes

When you're ready to take a walk, even a brief one, it's wise to give your body a signal that it's about to become active; this is especially important after you have been sitting (or standing) still for a while.

Do these before taking a walk (at lunch or coffee break) or before leaving the office at night. Also, do them *after* you walk.

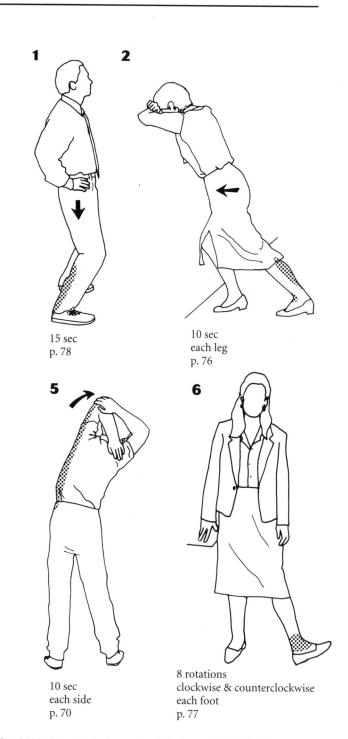

1

15 sec
p. 78

2

10 sec
each leg
p. 76

3

15 sec
each leg
p. 77

4

15 sec
p. 70

5

10 sec
each side
p. 70

6

8 rotations
clockwise & counterclockwise
each foot
p. 77

Stretching in the Office ©2002 Robert A. Anderson, Jean E. Anderson & Shelter Publications, Inc.

Adios! (Shut Down) Stretches

1 minute

Just as you take a few minutes in the morning to stretch while your computer is warming up, take 60 seconds after hitting "shut-down" before you leave the office.

- These stretches will help you shift out of the sitting mode and get you ready to move.
- Stretching is a signal to your muscles that they are about to be used.

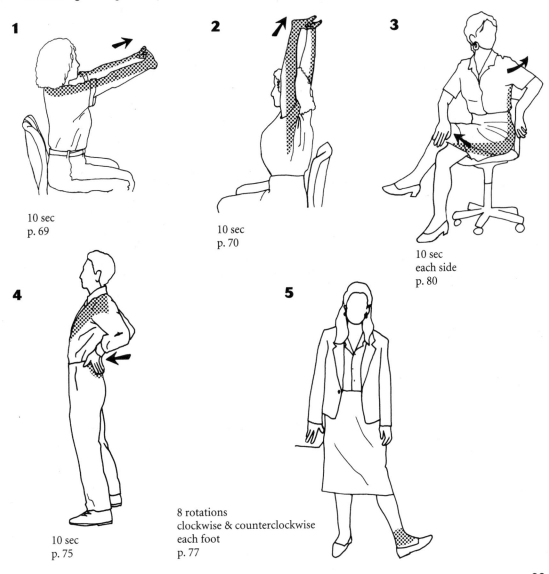

1

10 sec
p. 69

2

10 sec
p. 70

3

10 sec
each side
p. 80

4

10 sec
p. 75

5

8 rotations
clockwise & counterclockwise
each foot
p. 77

Sitting Stretches

During the hours we all spend sitting, it's beneficial to take the time to do these simple stretches. These can all be done sitting.

- Do in the order indicated.
- Do as many stretches as you like; you don't need to do them all.
- Stretch throughout the day.

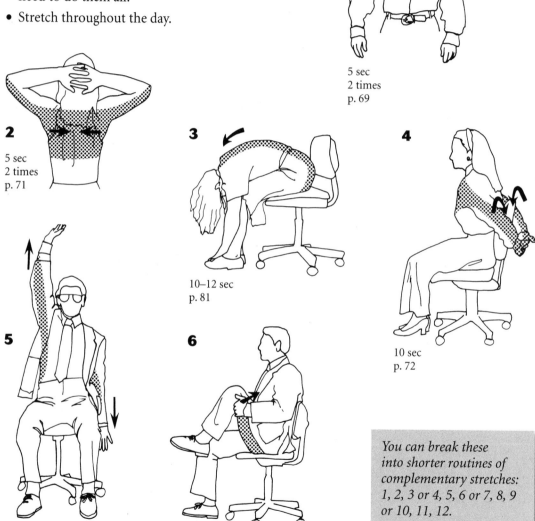

1

5 sec
2 times
p. 69

2

5 sec
2 times
p. 71

3

10–12 sec
p. 81

4

10 sec
p. 72

5

10 sec
each side
p. 73

6

15 sec
each leg
p. 79

You can break these into shorter routines of complementary stretches: 1, 2, 3 or 4, 5, 6 or 7, 8, 9 or 10, 11, 12.

7

15 sec
p. 70

8

10 sec
each arm
p. 71

9

10 sec
each side
p. 80

10

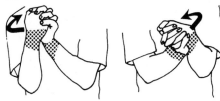

10 times
clockwise & counterclockwise
p. 65

11

10 sec
each position
p. 65

12

10 sec
shake hands
p. 68

Standing Stretches

(Stand & stretch whenever possible)

Standing stretches can improve circulation (especially in your feet and legs) and relieve the neck and back stiffness that comes from prolonged sitting. It's important to get up off your behind regularly throughout the day.

- Do in the order indicated.
- Do as many stretches as you like; you don't need to do them all.
- Stretch throughout the day.

1

5 sec
2 times
p. 81

2

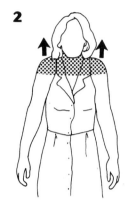

5 sec
2 times
p. 69

3

5 sec
each side
p. 73

4

15 sec
each side
p. 78

5

10 sec
each leg
p. 77

You can break these into shorter routines of complementary stretches: 1, 2, 3 or 4, 5, 6 or 7, 8, 9 or 10, 11, 12, 13.

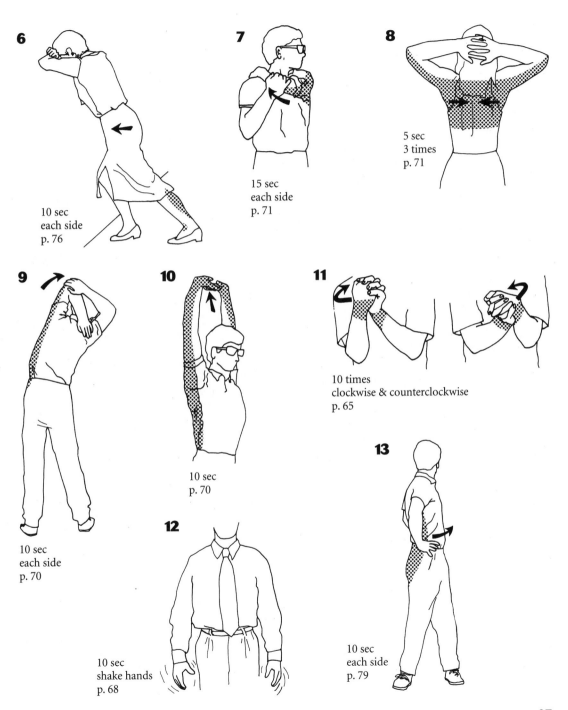

6

10 sec
each side
p. 76

7

15 sec
each side
p. 71

8

5 sec
3 times
p. 71

9

10 sec
each side
p. 70

10

10 sec
p. 70

11

10 times
clockwise & counterclockwise
p. 65

12

10 sec
shake hands
p. 68

13

10 sec
each side
p. 79

Sitting or Standing Stretches

Here is a combination of all-purpose sitting and standing stretches.

- Do in the order indicated.
- You don't have to do all these at one time; do as many stretches as you like.
- Stretch regularly throughout the day.
- Put a Post-it™ note on the bottom of your monitor as a reminder to stretch.

1

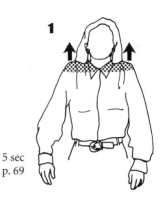

5 sec
p. 69

2

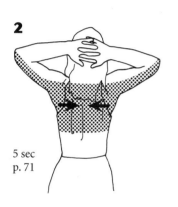

5 sec
p. 71

3

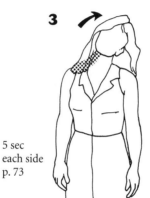

5 sec
each side
p. 73

4

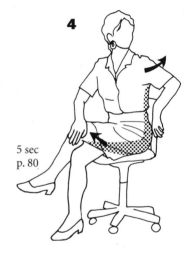

5 sec
p. 80

5

10 sec
p. 75

6

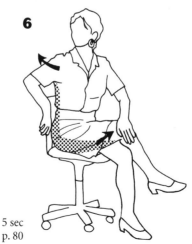

5 sec
p. 80

7

10 sec
each side
p. 71

Stretching in the Office ©2002 Robert A. Anderson, Jean E. Anderson & Shelter Publications, Inc.

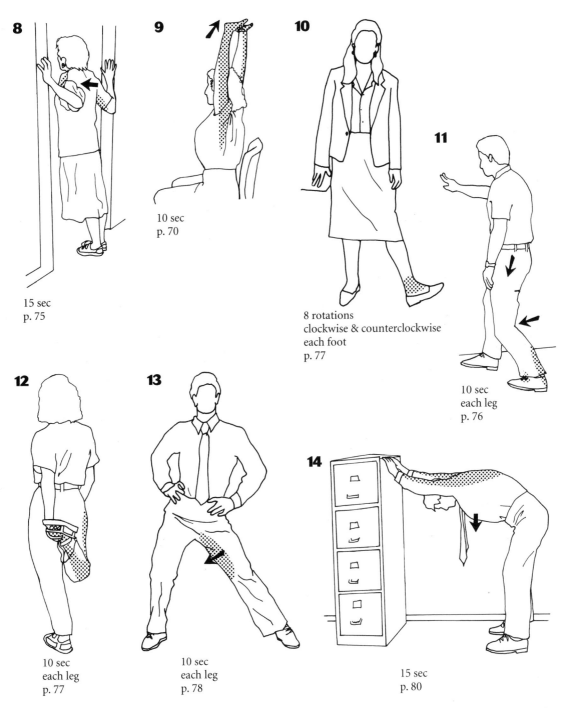

8

15 sec
p. 75

9

10 sec
p. 70

10

8 rotations
clockwise & counterclockwise
each foot
p. 77

11

10 sec
each leg
p. 76

12

10 sec
each leg
p. 77

13

10 sec
each leg
p. 78

14

15 sec
p. 80

No Gain with Pain

Hold only stretch tensions that feel good to you. Please, no forced painful stretches. They do more harm than good. The "no gain without pain" theory does not apply to stretching. Stretching *should not* be painful.

A Pain-Free Body

Repetitive Strain Injuries

epetitive strain injuries (RSIs) occur from repeated physical movements that damage tendons, nerves, muscles, or other soft body tissues. Unlike sudden injuries such as broken bones or a sore back from lifting something heavy, RSIs result from a gradual, continued accumulation of small, sometimes unnoticeable, changes that eventually produce pain.

Repetitive strain, or cumulative stress injuries, are nothing new. For years, meat packers, seamstresses, assembly line workers, and others in jobs requiring continuous, repetitive physical work — especially with their hands — suffered a variety of ailments. Athletes have always had RSIs, such as runner's knee or tennis elbow.

But in the last decade a completely new category of RSI has emerged: computer-related injuries — and the problem is enormous. It is estimated that some 50 million people in the United States now use computers, and many of them work on them longer than the safe limit of three hours daily. According to the U. S. Bureau of Labor Statistics, RSIs now account for over 60% of all workplace-related illnesses, and as we head ever further into the information economy, these problems are likely to get worse.

REMEMBER TYPEWRITERS?

In the days before word processors, typists did a greater variety of manual tasks — making corrections by hand, rolling a sheet of paper in and out of the carriage, manually returning the carriage, changing ribbons. Their hands moved in a variety of directions and the brief pauses gave the wrists a rest. With computers, however, these activities are automated. The operator may perform over 20,000 keystrokes in a single work period, with no variation and no "wrist rest" time.

ELECTRONIC INJURIES

Recent increases in computer usage and flat, light-touch keyboards that permit high-speed typing have resulted in an epidemic of injuries to the hands, arms, and shoulders. Pointing devices such as a mouse or a trackball are in large part responsible. Slowly, the thousands of repeated keystrokes and long periods of clutching and dragging with a mouse damage the body. Another name for these problems is Cumulative Trauma Disorder. This happens even more quickly due to improper keyboarding technique and/or body positions that place unnecessary stress on the tendons and nerves in the hand, wrist, arms, and even the shoulders and neck. Lack of adequate rest, not taking breaks, or using excessive force almost guarantee trouble.

CARPAL TUNNEL SYNDROME, ET AL

You may have heard the term *Carpal Tunnel Syndrome* (CTS) in connection with these injuries, but in fact CTS represents only a small and dangerous percentage of typing injuries. In his book *Repetitive Strain Injury,* Emil Pascarelli, M.D., states that DeQuervain's disease, involving acute pain at the junction of wrist and thumb, is a more common (if less known) problem than CTS. There are various types of tendinitis (shoulder, forearm, etc.), different forms of nerve damage, shoulder problems from holding the phone with one raised shoulder while typing, elbow and wrist problems from using the mouse, loss of circulation in the fingers, and different types of arthritis that may be aggravated by cumulative stress. All of these are serious and, in advanced cases, can cause great pain and permanent disability. It is not uncommon for people to have to leave computer-dependent careers as a result.

THINGS TO WATCH FOR

- Tightness, discomfort, stiffness, or pain in the hands, wrists, fingers, forearms, or elbows

- Tingling, coldness, or numbness in the hands

- Clumsiness or loss of strength and coordination in the hands

- Recurring pain in the neck or shoulders

- Pain that wakes you up at night

WHAT IF YOU HAVE SUCH SYMPTOMS?

We all have occasional aches and pains that go away in a day or two. But if you have recurring problems from using the computer, run, do not walk, to your doctor or health care provider *right away*. An early diagnosis is critical to limiting the damage, and may spare you a world of hurt, trouble, and frustration. You are not overreacting: by the time you have symptoms, some damage has already been done. If you try to ignore the pain, you may sustain a serious injury. If your doctor doesn't seem to know much about RSIs, find one who does. When you find one, listen to the diagnosis and get advice on any changes you intend to make or therapy you intend to try. There are no quick fixes. No wrist splint, arm rest, split keyboard, spinal adjustment, etc. is going to get you right back to work at full speed if you've been injured. Even carpal tunnel sufferers who undergo the release surgery on their wrists can be back in pain and trouble if they don't make long-term changes in the technique and work habits that hurt them in the first place. Healing *does* happen but it takes months, not days.

Ergonomic Principles

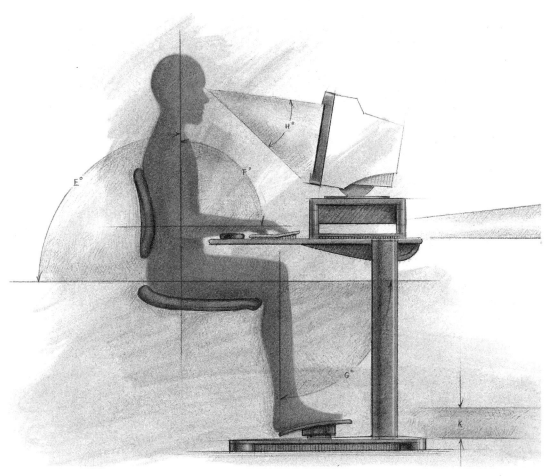

ERGONOMICS

The term *ergonomics* comes from the Greek words *ergos* meaning "work" and *nomos,* meaning "study of" or "natural laws of." The science of ergonomics dates back to the 1940s, but only in the past decade has it become a commonly known term. This is due to the recent epidemic of office-related injuries and the large body of equipment and information designed to solve these problems.

Modern-day office ergonomics is the science of providing furniture, tools, and equipment that improve the comfort, safety, and health of the office worker. We are not ergonomic experts, but we have studied the literature on the subject and there seem to be some basic principles on which most professionals agree. The following 4 pages contain some of the basics as an introduction to the subject.

SOME ERGONOMIC SPECIFICS

- **Monitor** should be an arm's length or a bit more from your eyes. Conventional ergonomic wisdom generally advises people that the center of the screen should be where their gaze falls naturally, with the top of the screen at eye level, and that the monitor should be tilted slightly to match the angle of one's gaze. A 1995 report, *Vision Comfort at VDTs,* by Stewart B. Leavitt, however, comes to a different conclusion: the monitor should be lower than this, in a *range* with the top about 15° below horizontal eye level to the lower limit where the bottom of the screen is 45° below eye level. If you are concerned about vision comfort and especially if you have eye problems such as blurring vision, burning eyes, or even neck and shoulder pain, we recommend that you read this detailed report. An adjustable stand or monitor riser (or homemade box) will allow you to make adjustments.

- **Keyboard** should be set at a height so that forearms, wrists, and hands are aligned when keyboarding, and parallel to the floor, or bent slightly down from elbow to hand—the hands are never bent back. Preferably the stand or desk on which the keyboard sits is adjustable. There are many "ergonomic" keyboards available, some of them quite unusual.

- **Mouse pad** should be at a height where your arm, wrist, and hand are aligned and in "neutral." It is best if the stand or desk the mouse pad sits on is adjustable.

- **Wrists,** while you are actually typing, should not rest on anything, and should not be bent up, down, or to the side. Your arms should move your hands around, and instead of resting your wrists, you should stretch to hit keys with your fingers. (There are wrist-rest devices on the market that give you a place to rest your hands, but only when pausing from typing, not *while* you are typing.)

- **Chair** should be adjustable and comfortable. Set it so that your thighs are either parallel to the floor or at a slight downward angle from the hips to the knees. You should sit straight, not slouching, and not straining forward to reach the keys. Stay relaxed. Anything that creates awkward reaches or angles in the body will create problems.

FURTHER TIPS

- **Align your wrists** Wrists also should not be bent to the side; instead your fingers should be in a straight line with your forearm, as viewed from above.

- **The proper keyboard angle** Research suggests that it may be better to tilt the back edge of your keyboard down, away from you. Put a prop an inch or two thick under the edge of the keyboard closest to you, but make sure the whole thing is still low enough so you aren't reaching up.

- **Frequently change positions** Movement is important during the working day. You may want to adjust the height or angle of your chair after a few hours, or to stand after sitting for a period. In fact, as reported in the ergonomic newsletter *OccuTrax* (Black Mountain, NC), "Ergonomic studies have verified that the least stressful working position is one where the individual can 'sit and stand' rather than sit 'or' stand."

- **Don't pound the keys** Use a light touch.

- **Use two hands to perform double-key operations** such as Command-P, Ctrl-C or Alt-F, instead of twisting one hand to do them. Move your whole hand to hit function keys with your strong fingers instead of stretching to reach them.

- **Hold the mouse lightly** Don't grip it hard or squeeze it. Place it where you don't have to reach up or over very far to use it (close to the keyboard is best). Better yet: learn and use equivalent keyboard commands whenever possible, as no pointing device is risk-free. Even trackballs have injured users.

- **Keep your arms and hands warm** Cold muscles and tendons are at much greater risk for overuse injuries, and many offices are overly air-conditioned.

- **Rest** When you stop typing for a while, rest your hands in your lap and/or on their sides instead of leaving them on the keyboard.

- **Stretch** Stretch frequently throughout the day *(see pages 52 to 55).*

- **Move** Get up and move whenever you can. If possible, walk to talk to a near-by colleague instead of using the phone. Try using the stairs (at least for some floors) instead of the elevator.

- **Take breaks** Holding utterly still is deadly. Some experts suggest a 10-second break every 3 minutes, others suggest a 1-minute break every 15 minutes, a 5-minute break every half hour, or a 15-minute break every 2 hours, etc. You can stretch and/or move around during these breaks.

- **Eliminate unnecessary computer usage.** No ergonomic changes, fancy keyboards, or exercises are going to help if you are typing more than your body can handle. Ask yourself: can some electronic-mail messages be replaced by telephone calls? How much time are you spending on the Internet? And watch it on the computer video games, which often involve long, unbroken sessions of very tense keyboard or controller use. If nothing else, *pause* the game every 3 to 4 minutes. Don't sacrifice your hands to a game!

TAKE CARE OF YOUR EYES

Anyone who operates a computer regularly would be wise to get a complete eye exam. Even minor sight defects should be corrected with lenses designed specifically for computer usage. Many computer operators, if they do not have to focus on distant objects while keyboarding, utilize bifocal lenses with the top calibrated for the computer screen and the bottom for reading. Or, if distant vision is required, the bifocals can have the top designed for distance and the bottom for the computer. Progressive lenses are also an option, where magnification is a gradient from top to bottom.

Glare on the screen should be avoided. A glare hood may help if there are overhead lights.Try to have any windows to the side, not in front of or behind the computer.

It's also very important to look up from the screen periodically and to focus on a distant object for a minute or two; do some stretches while doing this.

For further information see the description of Vision Comfort at VDTs— The Ergonomic Positioning of Monitors and Word Documents *on page 88.*

VOICE-RECOGNITION TECHNOLOGY

Voice recognitions systems allow you to input information with your voice or in conjunction with the keyboard and mouse. These entail software, and in some cases, hardware, and are very important for people who can no longer use a keyboard. (They can also be extremely useful while healing takes place.) *See references to the* Typing Injury FAQ Website *on page 91 in the Bibliography.*

THE ENVIRONMENT

Lighting, wall color, ventilation, reflections, electromagnetic fields, sounds, air quality, view, and other factors are all important considerations in an office environment. There are many sources of information on this topic you can investigate. *(See pp. 88 to 91 for resources.)*

WHAT CAN STRETCHING DO?

The author is not a doctor nor a specialist in injuries of any kind. However, from teaching people to stretch for over 20 years, he has seen the value of stretching in just about every area of physical activity. Here is what he would suggest:

• *If you are not injured,* use the stretches on pages 52 to 55 as preventative medicine. These are shoulder, neck, arm, hand, and wrist stretches. Stretch regularly throughout the day and you may be able to avoid RSI.

• *If you are injured,* take this book to your doctor or health care provider and ask which of the stretching programs you can follow. Point out that the stretching index on pages 94 to 95 can be used to customize a series of stretches for your particular condition.

THE VALUE OF EXERCISE

Exercise can help in just about every type of physical problem. For ideas on how to work some movement into your daily office schedule, see page 60.

FURTHER REFERENCE

On pages 88 to 91, we list books on RSI, ergonomics, catalogs with extensive product lines, and addresses for the large amount of information available on the Internet. You can also check the ads in your Yellow Pages under Office Furniture; look for the word "ergonomic."

Healing Takes Time

If you have a repetitive strain injury, don't expect an instant cure. Many people have found that after a few months of following good ergonomic principles *(see pp. 46 to 50)* and stretching regularly, their condition has improved.

Hand, Arm, Shoulder & Neck Stretches

(To Prevent Repetitive Strain Injuries)

Here is a series of stretches for the hands, arms, shoulders, and neck. If you have RSI-type problems, do not do any of these that cause pain. *Proceed with caution.*

If you do not have an RSI-type problem, we recommend you follow this routine as *preventive medicine.*

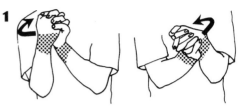

1

10 times
clockwise & counterclockwise
p. 65

2

5 sec
each arm
p. 66

3

pull each finger & thumb gently
4 times each direction
do both hands
p. 68

rotate each finger & thumb gently
4 times each direction
do both hands
p. 68

4

10 sec
each side
p. 73

5

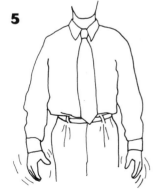

10 sec
shake hands
p. 68

6

5 sec
3 times
p. 69

52 *Stretching in the Office* ©2002 Robert A. Anderson, Jean E. Anderson & Shelter Publications, Inc.

- *Alternative.* You can do all 13 stretches in the order indicated; this will take 2 to 3 minutes. Or if you don't have time to do all of these at one time, you can break them into shorter routines of complementary stretches: 1, 2, 3 or 4, 5, 6, 7 or 8, 9,10 or 11, 12, 13.
- Frequently, the cause of wrist and hand problems is in the neck, shoulders or arms.
- The most important thing is to stretch regularly throughout the day.
- "An ounce of prevention . . ."

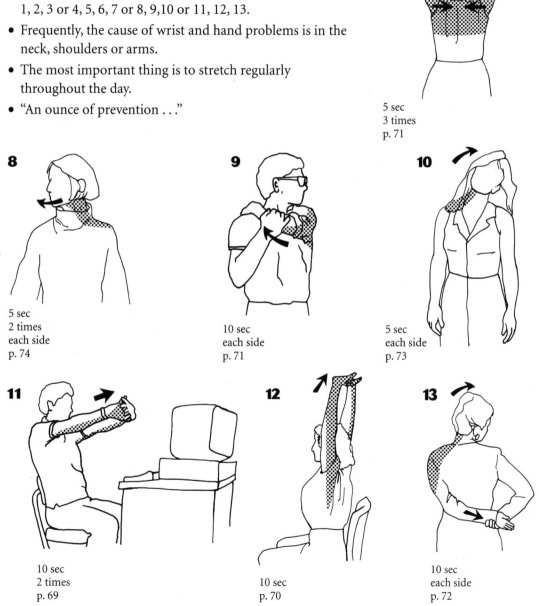

7

5 sec
3 times
p. 71

8

5 sec
2 times
each side
p. 74

9

10 sec
each side
p. 71

10

5 sec
each side
p. 73

11

10 sec
2 times
p. 69

12

10 sec
p. 70

13

10 sec
each side
p. 72

Hand, Wrist & Forearm Stretches

(To Prevent Repetitive Strain Injuries)

Here is a series of stretches for the hands, wrists and forearms. If you have RSI-type problems, do not do any of these that cause pain. *Proceed with caution.*

If you do not have an RSI-type problem, we recommend you follow this routine as *preventive medicine.*

1

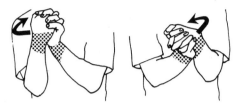

10 times
clockwise & counterclockwise
p. 65

2

10 sec
each position
p. 65

3

pull each finger & thumb gently
4 times each direction, do both hands
p. 68

rotate each finger & thumb gently
4 times each direction, do both hands
p. 68

4

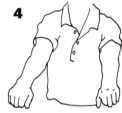

5 sec
2 times
p. 66

5

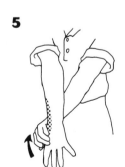

5 sec
each arm
p. 66

6

10 sec
shake hands
p. 68

7

10 sec
p. 67

Stretching in the Office ©2002 Robert A. Anderson, Jean E. Anderson & Shelter Publications, Inc.

Elapsed time: 40 seconds

Here is a special series of stretches for the wrists. You can do one or more of these at any time, especially while waiting a few seconds for the computer to process information. If you have wrist problems, do not do any of these that cause pain. If you do not have wrist problems, use these as *preventive medicine.*

- These are especially helpful stretches if you do a lot of keyboarding.
- Keep your wrists flexible and fingers supple.

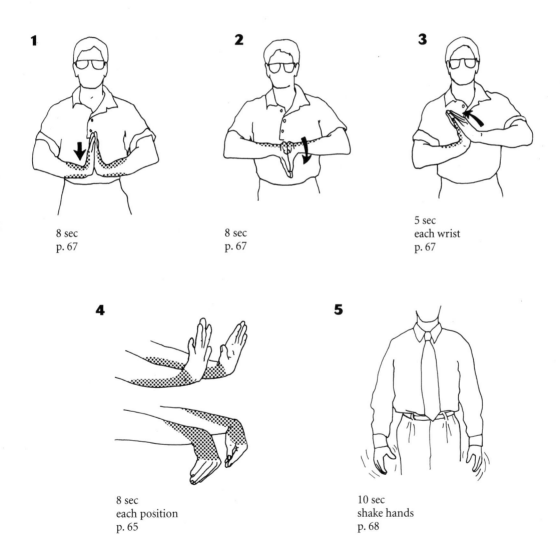

1

8 sec
p. 67

2

8 sec
p. 67

3

5 sec
each wrist
p. 67

4

8 sec
each position
p. 65

5

10 sec
shake hands
p. 68

Good Habits for a Pain-Free Body

Posture and body position are extremely important in anything you do. Here are some brief tips on sitting, standing, and lifting. Open the book to these pages every so often and practice these suggestions until you eventually train your body to do them automatically.

Wrong · Right

Sitting Posture

An "ergonomic" chair with a firm back and support enables you to maintain the lumbar curve in your low back. Set the chair at a proper level so that your knees are level when both feet are flat on floor. Don't cross your legs. Don't lean forward or slouch. Note: crossing your ankles is better for circulation than crossing your knees. (See page 46 for more information on sitting.)

Standing Posture

- When standing, bend knees slightly; don't lock knees — keeping them slightly bent gives you some spring, some flex.
- Use your quadriceps muscles to control your posture when standing. This is a position of power.
- Keeping your pelvis slightly pushed forward and your stomach tucked in will help prevent lower back pain.
- Imagine a string coming out of the top of your head and from which you hang; this helps you visualize proper alignment.

Stretching in the Office ©2002 Robert A. Anderson, Jean E. Anderson & Shelter Publications, Inc.

Standing

When you stand in one place for a period of time, prop one foot up on a box or a short stool. Alternate your feet often. This will relieve some of the back tension that comes from prolonged standing.

Lifting

- Hold the lifted load close to your body. The closer you hold it, the less stress on your back.
- Keep your back upright during the lift.
- Bend your knees and minimize any bending at the waist. Bending at the waist, with legs straight, greatly increases the strain on your back.
- Lift with your legs by slowly straightening them. Make your legs do the work, not your back.
- Don't twist while lifting.

Office Exercises

By Bill Pearl

Sitting much of the day causes loss of muscle tone due to inactivity. Here are a few light muscle-strengthening exercises from four-time Mr. Universe Bill Pearl. They can be done in the office with no equipment. (This is weight training without the weights—using only your body weight.) Use your imagination for other things you can do.

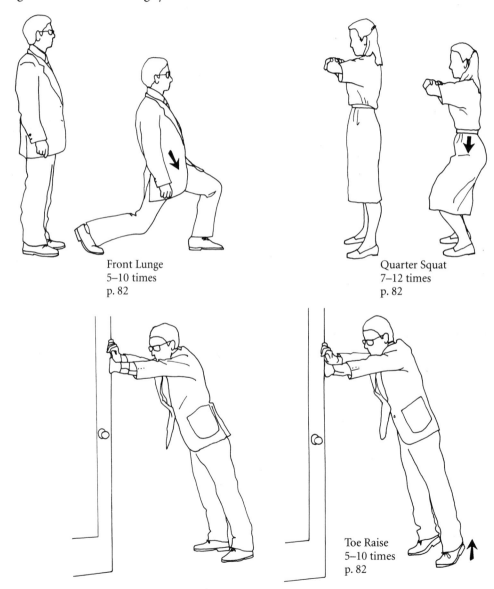

Front Lunge
5–10 times
p. 82

Quarter Squat
7–12 times
p. 82

Toe Raise
5–10 times
p. 82

Stretching in the Office ©2002 Robert A. Anderson, Jean E. Anderson & Shelter Publications, Inc.

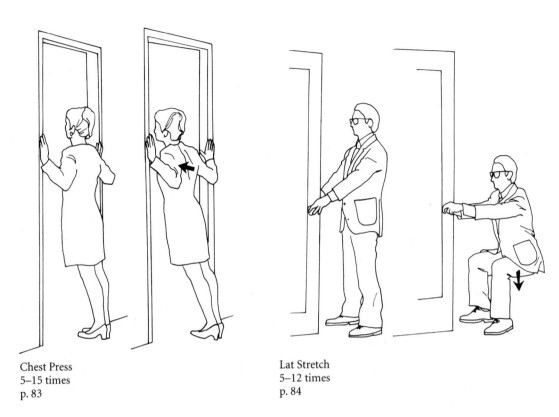

Chest Press
5–15 times
p. 83

Lat Stretch
5–12 times
p. 84

Desk Pushup
2–10 times
p. 84

Moving

THE ANTIDOTE FOR SITTING

Sitting for long periods is a very recent phenomenon in human history. Many health problems of the modern world are either caused by or aggravated by the sedentary life.

In recent years, exercise has been shown to have beneficial effects for a variety of medical problems. From arthritis to back pain (the recommendation used to be "stay in bed") to osteoporosis to cancer. Likewise, moving exercise can help decrease the chances of contracting office-related injuries and, if done sensibly, can help heal symptoms and speed recovery.

THE NEW APPROACH

In the last two decades, there has been an overemphasis on strenuous workouts in America. Running marathons, intense aerobic dance classes, competitive cycling, and swimming were often touted as necessary for good health. Experience has shown, however, that most people will not stick with an exercise program that is too strenuous. More recent studies show that even mild exercise, such as walking 10 minutes a day, can do a world of good. Or as Dr. Steven Blair puts it in his book *Living With Exercise*, "Standing is better than sitting, moving is better than standing . . ." If you have been sedentary for some time, try walking 5 minutes; then the next day 6 minutes, and so on. Or walk around the house during TV commercials.

Here are a few ideas for building some physical activity into your daily life.

ON THE JOB

- *Take mini-walks* Walk during coffee breaks. Arrange a walk-and-talk instead of a sit-and-talk meeting.

- *Climb stairs* Walk at least some of the distance up or down in office buildings.

- *Park and walk* Park farther away from the office (or the store when shopping), instead of trying to get as close as possible.

- *Walk on your lunch break* You'll return refreshed. Wear comfortable shoes.

- *Move while on the phone* Stand and move around while talking on the phone. Do some stretches. *(See p. 31.)*

- Swing your arms, turn your neck, or wiggle your toes—any kind of movement helps.

OFF THE JOB

Use off-the-job time to exercise neglected muscles rather than straining those that are already overworked. Be creative.

- **_Walking_** is now the most popular form of exercise in America. It can be done practically anytime, anywhere and all you need is a good pair of shoes.

- **_Walk with the kid(s)_** when babysitting.

- **_Games_** are a great way to exercise. Softball, volleyball, bowling, tennis, any of these things you do for fun and socializing will get your circulation going.

- **_Dancing_** is also great exercise and fun.

- **_House and garden work_** such as mowing the lawn, vacuuming the house, washing the car, etc. are all moving exercise.

- **_Regular exercise_** Any typical endurance activity such as running, cycling, swimming, especially if done 3 times a week, will do you a world of good.

Stretch and Move at Work So You Have a Life When You Get Home

Many people feel awful after work and don't feel like doing anything then. However, if you can stretch, and do a little walking or other exercise in the office, you'll feel better when you get home. You'll have more energy to do things that are fun and/or fitness-oriented.

Stretching Instructions

Detailed Instructions on How to Do Each Stretch

In this section there are 43 different stretches and exercises with detailed instructions telling you how to do each one. It's important to know the proper procedures and positions for the stretches, even though they are simple. You'll get the full benefits of stretching by doing the stretches correctly.

- Each stretch in the routines *(pp. 19 to 55)* has a page number reference to these instructions.

- Refer to the instructions until you know what to do for each stretch. From then on, you'll only have to look at the figures in the programs.

- *An alternative to the routines:* You can also follow through these instructions, one after the other, rather than using the routines on pages 19 to 55.

- **Note:** *The shading in each drawing shows those areas of the body where you will most likely feel the stretch.*

- Separate and straighten your fingers until the tension of a stretch is felt
- Hold 10 seconds
- Relax, then bend fingers at the knuckles and hold 10 seconds
- Repeat the first stretch once more

Stretches hands, fingers, and wrists

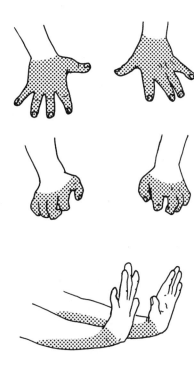

- With arms extended, palms down, bend your wrists and raise your finger-tips
- Hold 10 seconds
- Now bend your wrists back in the opposite direction, fingers pointing down
- Hold 10 seconds

Stretches wrists and lower arms

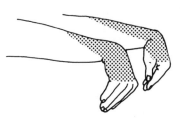

- Interlace your fingers in front of you
- Rotate your hands and wrists clockwise 10 times
- Repeat counterclockwise 10 times

Stretches wrists

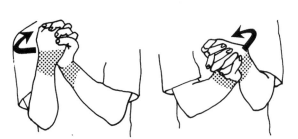

- With right arm held straight out, turn palm of hand up
- Reach under forearm with your left hand and hold your thumb and inside of palm
- With your left hand, slowly turn your right hand out and down until you feel a mild stretch
- Hold 5–10 seconds
- Repeat for other arm

Stretches wrists and forearms

- Arms straight out in front
- Slowly turn your hands to the outside until a stretch is felt
- Hold 5–10 seconds

Stretches wrists and forearms

- Place your hands palm-to-palm in front of you
- Move hands downward, keeping your palms together, until you feel a mild stretch
- Keep elbows up and even
- Hold 5–8 seconds

Stretches wrists, forearms, and hands

- From above stretch, rotate palms around until they face more or less downward
- Go until you feel a mild stretch
- Keep elbows up and even
- Hold 5–8 seconds

Stretches wrists, forearms, and hands

- Place your hands palm-to-palm in front of you
- Push one hand gently to the side until you feel a mild stretch
- Keep elbows up and even
- Hold 5–8 seconds

Stretches wrists, forearms, and hands

Hands

- Hold the index finger of your opposite hand
- Rotate 5 times clockwise, then 5 times counterclockwise
- Rotate each finger and thumb

Stretches fingers

- Next, gently pull your finger straight out and hold 2–3 seconds
- Do the same thing with each finger and thumb
- Repeat for your other hand

Stretches fingers

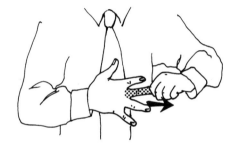

- Shake your arms and hands at your sides 10–12 seconds
- Keep your jaw relaxed and let shoulders hang downward as you shake out the tension

Increases circulation

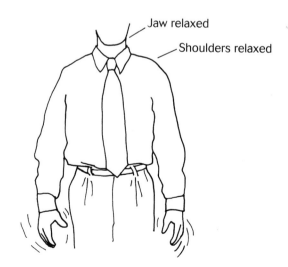

Jaw relaxed

Shoulders relaxed

- Interlace your fingers, then straighten your arms out in front of you

- Palms should be facing away from you

- Feel the stretch in your arms and through the upper part of your back (shoulder blades)

- Hold stretch 10 seconds

Stretches shoulders, arms, wrists, and fingers

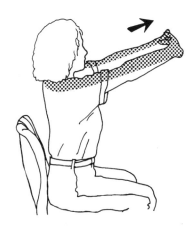

This is a good stretch to use at the first signs of tightness or tension in the shoulder and neck area.

- Raise the top of your shoulders toward your ears until you feel a slight tension in your neck and shoulders

- Hold this 3–5 seconds, then relax your shoulders downward into normal position

- Think: "shoulders hang, shoulders down"

Stretches shoulders and neck

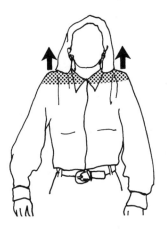

- Hold your left elbow with your right hand
- Gently pull your elbow behind your head until an easy tension-stretch is felt in shoulder or back of your upper arm (triceps)
- Hold easy stretch 10 seconds
- Don't overstretch or hold breath
- Do both sides

Stretches triceps, top of shoulders, and sides

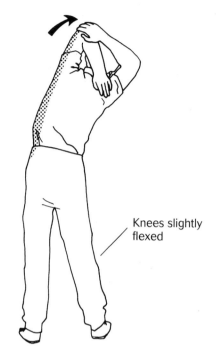

Knees slightly flexed

- Interlace your fingers, then turn your palms upward above your head as you straighten your arms
- Think of elongating your arms as you feel a stretch through your arms and upper sides of your rib cage
- Hold 10–15 seconds
- Excellent for slumping shoulders
- Breathe deeply

Stretches shoulders, back, arms, and hands

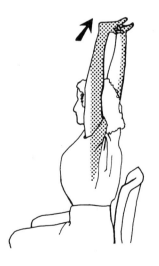

- With fingers interlaced behind your head, keep your elbows straight out to the side with your upper body erect

- Now pull your shoulder blades toward each other to create a feeling of tension through your upper back and shoulder blades

- Hold 5 seconds, then relax

Stretches shoulders, chest, and upper back

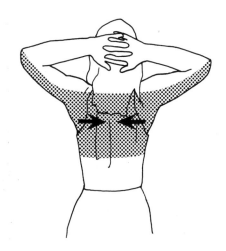

- Hold your left arm just above your elbow with your right hand

- As you look over your left shoulder, gently pull your elbow toward the opposite shoulder until a stretch is felt

- Hold 10–15 seconds

- Do both sides

Stretches sides of shoulders, back of upper arms, and neck

Shoulders & Arms

- Interlace your fingers behind your back, palms facing your back
- Slowly turn your elbows inward while straightening your arms until a stretch is felt
- Lift your breast bone slightly upward as you stretch
- Hold 10 seconds

Stretches arms, chest, hands, and shoulders

- With your right hand, gently pull your left arm gently down and across, behind your back
- Lean your head sideways toward the right shoulder
- Hold 10 seconds
- Repeat other side
- Relax

Stretches top of shoulders and neck

Shoulders, Arms & Neck

- Extend your right arm above your head
- Reach down with your left arm as you reach up with your right arm
- Point your fingers
- Hold 10 seconds
- Repeat other side
- If you do this stretch standing, keep your knees slightly flexed
- Breathe easily

Stretches shoulders and arms

- Sit or stand, arms hanging loosely at your sides
- Tilt your head sideways, first to one side, then the other
- Keep your shoulders relaxed downward during the stretch
- Hold 5 seconds each side

Stretches sides of neck

Neck & Shoulders

- Sit or stand with your arms hanging loosely at your sides
- Gently tilt your head forward to stretch the back of your neck
- Keep your shoulders relaxed downward
- Hold 5 seconds

Stretches neck

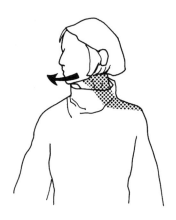

- Sit or stand with your arms hanging loosely at your sides
- Turn your head to one side, then to the other
- Hold 5 seconds, each side

Stretches sides of neck

- Place hands just above the back of your hips, elbows back
- Gently press forward
- Slightly lift your breast bone upward as you hold the stretch
- Hold 10–15 seconds
- Breathe easily
- *Note: can also be done sitting*

Stretches chest and back

- Place your hands at shoulder-height on either side of a doorway
- Move your upper body forward until you feel a comfortable stretch
- Keep your chest and head up, your knees slightly bent
- Hold 15 seconds
- Breathe easily

Stretches chest and inside of upper arms

Legs

- Stand a little way from a wall and lean on it with your forearms, head resting on your hands

- Place your right foot in front of you, your leg bent, your left leg straight behind you

- Slowly move your hips forward until you feel a stretch in the calf of your left leg

- Keep your left heel flat and toes pointed straight ahead

- Hold easy stretch 10–20 seconds

- Do not bounce

- Repeat other leg

Stretches calves

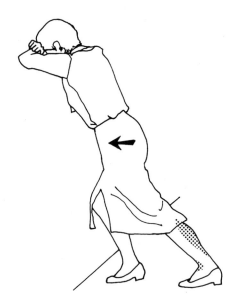

- From the previous stretch, lower your hips downward

- Slightly bend your left knee, keeping your back flat

- Keep your left foot slightly toed-in or straight, heel down

- Hold 10 seconds

- Repeat other leg

Stretches calves, Achilles area, and ankles

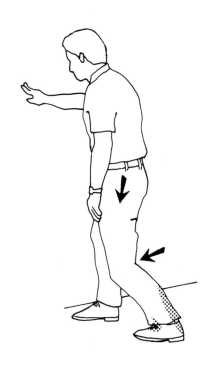

- Stand and hold onto something for balance
- Lift your left foot and rotate foot and ankle 8–10 times clockwise, then 8–10 times counterclockwise
- Repeat other side
- *Note: can also be done sitting*

Stretches ankles and improves circulation

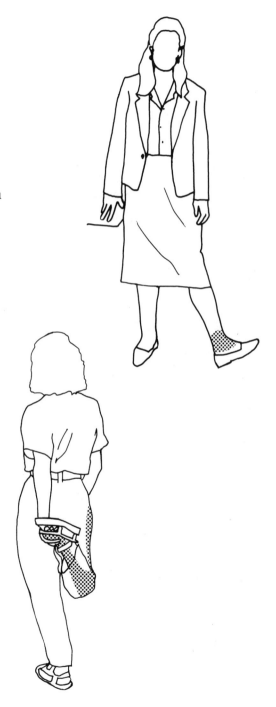

- Place your right hand on something for support (e.g., wall or chair)
- Standing straight, grasp the top of your right foot with your left hand
- Gently pull your heel toward your buttock until a slight stretch is felt
- Hold 10–20 seconds
- Repeat for other leg

Stretches front of thighs (quadriceps), ankles, and knees

- Stand with your feet shoulder-width apart
- Keep your heels flat, toes pointed straight ahead
- Assume a bent knee position (quarter squat)
- Hold 20–30 seconds

Stretches calves, Achilles area, and ankles; relaxes hamstrings

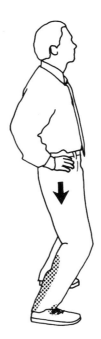

- Stand with your feet pointed straight ahead, a little more than shoulder-width apart
- Bend your left knee slightly and move your right hip downward toward your right knee
- Hold 10–15 seconds
- Repeat for the other leg

Stretches inner thighs and groin

- Sitting, hold onto your upper left leg just above and behind the knee
- Gently pull your bent leg toward your chest
- Hold 10–15 seconds
- Repeat other side

Stretches hamstrings and lower back

- Stand with hands on your hips
- Gently turn your torso at the waist and look over your shoulder until you feel the stretch
- Hold 8–10 seconds
- Repeat other side
- Keep your knees slightly flexed
- Do not hold your breath

Stretches back and sides

- Sit with your left leg bent over your right leg
- Rest the hand of your right arm on the outside of your upper left thigh
- Apply steady, controlled pressure toward the right with your hand
- As you do this, look over your left shoulder and feel the stretch
- Hold 5–10 seconds
- Repeat other side
- Breathe slowly

Stretches lower back, side of hip, and neck

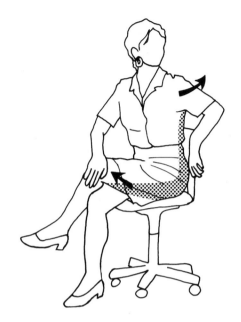

- Place your hands shoulder-width apart on a file cabinet or the wall
- Bend your knees; hips directly above feet
- Lower your head between your arms
- Hold stretch 10–15 seconds

Stretches neck, shoulders, arms, upper back

- Lean forward to stretch
- Keep your head down and your neck relaxed
- Hold 10–20 seconds
- Use your hands to push yourself upright

Stretches back

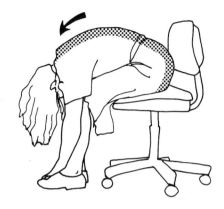

Face

- Raise your eyebrows and open your eyes wide
- At the same time, open your mouth to stretch your facial muscles
- Hold 5 seconds

Relaxes face, relieves jaw tension (and makes other people laugh!)

Office Exercises

Front Lunge

- Head up, back straight, feet 6 inches apart
- Step forward as shown
- Return to standing position
- Try to keep back leg straight
- Repeat with other leg

Quarter Squat

- Arms crossed in front of chest
- Head up, back straight, feet 16 inches apart
- Squat as shown
- Return to standing position

Chest Press

- Stand with hands against a door jamb
- Feet shoulder-width apart
- Lean forward, bending arms at elbows
- Press back to standing position

Toe Raise

- Stand about 40 inches from a door or the wall
- Lean forward, arms crossed
- Back straight, head up, legs locked
- Rise on toes as high as possible
- Come back down

Office Exercises

Squat

- Holding onto doorknobs, stand straight, feet shoulder-width apart
- Bend knees and squat (only as far as is comfortable)
- Return to standing position
- Keep arms straight

Desk Pushup

- Feet together, hand on desk at arm's length
- Inhale and press forward, bending arms at elbows
- Legs straight, heels down
- Return to standing position and exhale

It Couldn't Be Simpler

Remember: You can stretch anywhere, any time. Indoors or out, no special clothes needed. No classes to attend, no teacher required . . .

Appendix

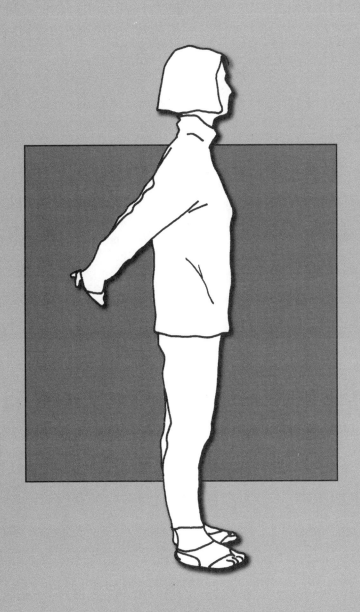

Bibliography

Rather than present a long list of reference material, we have selected the best books, newsletters, catalogs, and Web sites on the subject and reviewed them here for your convenience.

BOOKS ON ERGONOMICS

Comfort at Your Computer by Paul Linden (North Atlantic Books: Berkeley, CA, 2000).

A practical book with exercises for preventing computer stress, tips on posture, proper sitting, healthy functioning of various body parts, and detailed descriptions of setting up a workstation. The author does not agree with many commonly accepted ergonomic principles and offers unique tips on adjusting and even building a workstation tailor-made to your needs. This is perhaps the best book out there on using the body in a stress-free and comfortable way and for customizing a workstation. There is a section on how to work with a drawing tablet, how to use a laptop, and setting up a standing workstation. A unique and detailed approach.

25 Steps to Safe Computing by Don Sellers (Peachpit Press: Berkeley, CA, 1995).

A small, slim volume from the computer gurus at Peachpit Press. Information is in bite-sized bits, clear, and readily accessible. An excellent (and inexpensive) guide for employers to give to each employee to foster safe computing habits. It's simple, well researched, helpful, easy to understand, and particularly suited to today's busy lifestyle. Covers the basics on office health, how to keep the body functioning, safe workstations, finding the right doctor, and the subject of pregnancy and computing. Keep it in your desk.

BOOKS ON INJURIES

Conquering Carpal Tunnel Syndrome by Sharon J. Butler (Advanced Press, Berwyn, PA, 1995).

Over 40 stretches and exercises for people with repetitive strain injuries. There is a cross-reference from the type problem (tingling fingers, painful elbows, etc.) to the exercises designed to alleviate the condition. There is also a chart of professions with recommended exercises for each group; one set of exercises for architects and dental hygenists, another set for carpenters and guitarists, etc. A unique feature is the number of stretches for wrists hands, fingers, and thumbs. The author practices Hellerwork, an offshoot of Rolfing, and stresses freeing up the body's connective tissue, or myofascia, to restore it to a more normal state, thereby regaining flexibility and range of motion.

Listen to Your Pain: The Active Person's Guide to Understanding, Identifying and Treating Pain and Injury by Ben E. Benjamin, Ph.D. (Penguin Books, New York, NY, 1984).

This is a book primarily for injured athletes, but it is also the best book available on injuries in general, whether they come from sports, accidents, or gradual wear and tear. (An exception is that it does not cover hand, wrist, or forearm problems.) It is divided up by body parts and gives you unique methods for self-diagnosis to identify what the injury is, followed with step-by-step remedies to facilitate healing. An excellent reference book for the home library.

Repetitive Strain Injury: A Computer User's Guide by Emil Pascarelli, M.D., and Deborah Quilter (John Wiley & Sons, New York, NY, 1994).

One of the best books on RSI, written by a doctor with a great deal of experience—he has worked with over 1,000 injured people, many of them musicians. He calls RSI "a preventable tragedy," describes the warning signs, classifies different types of RSI (the latter is particularly concise and informative), explains treatment options, and talks about setting up the workstation. There is a good section called "The Road to Recovery," with advice on dealing with a doctor, self care, working during the recovery phase, activities of daily living, and preventing further injuries.

Treat Your Own Back by Robin McKenzie (Spinal Publications: Waikanae, New Zealand, 1981)

A book dedicated to the McKenzie method of treatment for back pain. The book contains background information on the spine, in particular the lumbar region and problems with mechanical back pain. There is information on the common causes of back pain, including sitting for prolonged periods, working in a stooped position, incorrect lifting technique, prolonged standing, and even coughing and sneezing. McKenzie illustrates several exercises for the relief of pain, explains when to apply the exercises, and includes special instructions for pregnant women and people with osteoporosis. There is even a "Panic Page" for onset of acute pain.

Treat Your Own Neck by Robin McKenzie (Spinal Publications: Waikanae, New Zealand, 1981)

A companion volume to *Treat Your Own Back* in which author Robin McKenzie explains the causes, and treatment through special exercise, of pain related to the neck.

End Your Carpal Tunnel Pain Without Surgery: A Daily Program to Prevent and Treat Carpal Tunnel Syndrome by Kate Montgomery (Rutledge Hill Press: Nashville, Tennessee, 1998)

This helpful guide tells how to prevent and treat carpal tunnel syndrome in just fifteen minutes a day. The author claims that a twelve-step routine of adjustments, stretches, and exercises can eliminate CTS pain without surgery. This book features information on how to tell if you have carpal tunnel syndrome, how to get instant relief from pain, why drug treatments don't work, and how to create a safe, pain-free workplace.

BOOKS ON GENERAL FITNESS

Stretching–Revised edition by Bob Anderson; illustrated by Jean Anderson (Shelter Publications, Bolinas, CA, 2000).

One of the most popular fitness books in the world, with over 3½ million copies sold and translated into 27 languages. A clear, readable, graphic summary of 200 different stretches with 1- and 2-page routines for everyday stretches, TV stretches, stretches for lower back pain, to do after sitting, before walking, as well as stretching programs for over 20 sports. There is a "Stretching & Exercise Prescriptions" index in the back of the book that can be used by readers or medical professionals to design customized stretching programs.

Getting in Shape by Bob Anderson, Bill Pearl and Ed Burke; illustrated by Jean Anderson (Shelter Publications, Bolinas, CA, 2002).

A unique and comprehensive workout book for people who want to get back into shape. The authors feel that most fitness books are too ambitious for the average person and have produced a book that can be tailor-made to each person's individual condition. There is a series of graphic programs starting with the 3-stage "Program Before the Program" designed to get you started when you're out of shape. There are 30 programs overall, each with the 3 components of fitness: stretching, weightlifting, and moving exercise. A simple, easy to follow, and visual approach to lifetime fitness, especially useful for the over-40 adult.

Bibliography

RSI NEWSLETTERS

CTD News
P.O. Box 980, Horsham, PA 19044-0980
(800-341-7874)
www.ctdnews.com
 Monthly newsletter aimed at businesses concerned with repetitive strain injuries or cumulative trauma disorders and giving up-to-date news on ergonomic safety. For example, a recent issue covered the relatively new use of angioplasty in CTS to stretch wrist and hand ligaments, thereby bypassing the need for surgery. Free samples of newsletter sent upon request.

RSI Newsletter
http://www.safecomputing.com/
 Available only on the Web, this is a newsletter of interest to people who have repetitive strain injuries. Information on ergonomic safety.

ERGONOMIC CATALOGS

AliMed Ergonomic Products
P.O. Box 9135, Dedham, MA, 02027-9135
(800-225-2610)
www.alimed.com
 Large catalog of wrist straps, many other ergonomic office products, mainly for professionals. They publish a shorter magazine called *Ergonomics and Occupational Health.*

Fellowes Computerware
1789 Norwood Ave., Itasca, IL, 60143
(800-456-1289)
www.fellowes.com
 Fellowes manufactures over 400 computer accessory products — wrist rests, monitor filters, seating supports, copy stands, adjustable monitor arms, cordless mouse pens, etc., many of them original design. They have an ergonomic task force that specializes in working with corporations interested in safe ergonomic practices. A complete list of products available upon request.

The North American Ergonomic Resources Guide
Published by CTD News,
P.O. Box 980, Horsham, PA 19044-0980
(800-341-7874)
 This is an excellent compendium of information on all aspects of ergonomics: a listing of many catalogs of ergonomic products and furniture; alternative keyboards and mice, voice control systems, books, videos, software, other resources. There are also nationwide lists of ergonomic consultants, educational conferences, and databases.

Saunders Ergosource
4250 Noprex Dr., Chaska MN 55318-3047
(800-969-4374)
 Catalog of ergonomic aids, tools, furniture, and educational literature.

Upper Extremity Technology Products
UE Tech, 2001 Blake Ave., 2-A,
Glenwood Springs, CO 81601
(800-736-1894)
www.uetech.com
 Catalog contains a number of books on repetitive motion injuries, ergonomic design, rehabilitation, etc. "By therapists . . . for therapists."

WORLDWIDE WEB

Computer-Related Repetitive Strain Injury
http://www.engr.unl.edu/ee/eeshop/rsi.html
 This is an excellent site for sound ergonomic principles and the basics of RSI without being boring or academic. Webmaster Paul Marxhausen has had RSI problems since 1994 and urges people with any of the listed symptoms to ". . . run, do not walk, to your doctor or health care provider *right away.*" He is aware of the value of early diagnosis and treatment. There are links to other sites, products, and resources, including "FindADoc," aimed at locating doctors specializing in RSI throughout the country.

Typing Injury FAQ:
A Guide to Comfortable Computing
www.tifaq.com

This is the granddaddy of online RSI information sites. Tons of information here, with links going off in many directions to all kinds of data on the subject. Lots of info on products such as keyboards, alternative pointing devices, desks and chairs, a very complete list of various software programs that will remind you to stretch while at the keyboard, and an archive of typing injuries.

Shelter Online

http://www.shelterpub.com

Shelter Publications' website, with information on stretching, (including—ahem!—programs from this book), weight training, running, fitness in general, healthy cooking, and a variety of other subjects.

INTERNET NEWSGROUPS

Sorehand

A very active newsgroup of people with computer-related problems. These are the people in the trenches. If you subscribe, be forewarned, you will get a ton of e-mail. Much of it is helpful and up-to-date—an example of the unique facility of Internet information exchange. The irony is that the helpful data comes to you through the same device that is causing the trouble.

To subscribe, send message "subscribe sorehand <your name>" to: listserv@itssrvl.ucsf.edu

C+health

Another excellent source of info on RSI, with contributors from around the world. There's something unique and especially relevant about these personal accounts from many people with the same problems. The network of people helping one another is useful as well as inspiring, and the exchanges are more current than is available in any other media.

To subscribe, send message "subscribe c+health <your name>" to: listserv@iubvm.ucs.indiana.edu

Body Tools

Sometimes you need a helping hand—or a helping tool—to make you feel better. Listed on these two pages are body tools that can be used for self-massage and loosening up in the office. They help relieve pain and tension. All but The Back Revolution® can be kept in or on your desk.

TheraCane®: acupressure tool. Loosens tight, painful areas—creates the pressure you want. Excellent for mid-back (between shoulder blades), sides of neck, shoulders.

Chinese Balls: exercise for your hands. Rotating balls in one direction, then another develops small muscles of hands, improves arm circulation, may help prevent carpal tunnel syndrome.

Trigger Wheel®: 2-inch nylon wheel on 4½-inch handle for deep massage. Works on trigger points of muscles. Can use directly on skin or through light clothing. It works the way a tire rolls back and forth on the pavement.

Knobble®: small hand tool for doing deep tissue massage or pressure point release. Saves wear and tear on your hands. Made of solid maple.

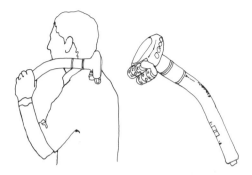

The Pain Eraser 1®: An exceptional hand-held tool that is firm enough for deep massage and yet soft enough for the most tender parts of your body, including your face. Access arms, legs, hands, feet, back, etc. easily with this high quality massage tool. 1½"-wide roller is made of 100% natural rubber with 36 "fingers."

Panasonic Reach Easy®: A gentle multi-surfaced rechargeable massager, perfect for people who want gentle, but effective relief from muscle tension with cordless convenience.

See p. M-37 for information on ordering any of these tools.

The Foot Massage®: 2 inches by 9 inches, with raised knobs of hard rubber for foot massage and rubber rings to protect floors. Super tool for tired feet.

The Back Revolution®: Truly a revolution, much better than hanging by heels, this stretches spine, decompresses discs and works wonders for sore, stiff necks. Benefits accrue from using it only 1 to 2 times daily.

Index of Stretches

Here are all the stretches in the book. This allows you to select stretches by body part. It can also serve as a guide for health care professionals in prescribing individual fitness or rehabilitation programs. Make a copy of this and circle the prescribed stretches.

Hands & Wrists   pp. 65–68

Shoulders & Arms   pp. 69–73

Shoulders & Arms *(cont'd)*

Neck & Shoulders   pp. 73–74

Chest   p. 75

Legs   pp. 76–78

Back   pp. 79–81

Stretching in the Office ©2002 Robert A. Anderson, Jean E. Anderson & Shelter Publications, Inc.

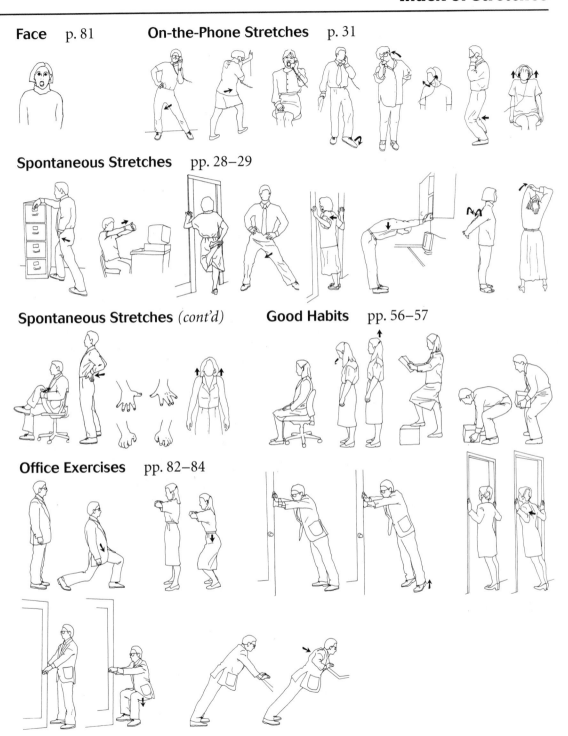

Face   p. 81

On-the-Phone Stretches   p. 31

Spontaneous Stretches   pp. 28–29

Spontaneous Stretches *(cont'd)*

Good Habits   pp. 56–57

Office Exercises   pp. 82–84

Stretching in the Office ©2002 Robert A. Anderson, Jean E. Anderson & Shelter Publications, Inc.

Index

Note: Page numbers in italics refer to illustrations.

About the Authors

Bob Anderson is the author of *Stretching,* which has sold over 3½ million copies worldwide and is in 27 languages.* Bob was born in Fullerton, California, and is a graduate of California State University at Long Beach with a lifetime credential in physical education. These days, Bob travels around the country, appearing at medical clinics, health conventions, training camps, and fitness centers. His appearances generally involve getting (himself and audience) down on the floor and doing a series of gentle stretches. All the while Bob talks about good health and the importance of keeping one's body strong and flexible and keeping the heart and cardiovascular system in good shape.

Bob is fit and healthy these days, but it wasn't always so. In 1968, he was overweight (190 pounds—at 5 feet 9 inches) and out of shape. He began a personal fitness program that got him down to 135 pounds. Yet one day, while in a physical conditioning class in college, he found he couldn't reach much past his knees in a straight-legged sitting position. So Bob started stretching. He found he soon felt better and that stretching made his running and cycling easier.

Since that time, Bob has continued to practice what he preaches. He spends several hours each day running on the steep mountain trails above his house in Colorado and riding his mountain bike. He has run the Catalina Island Marathon in Southern California, the Pikes Peak Marathon 10 years in a row, and regularly runs the 18-mile Imogen Pass Run, a mountain race from Ouray to Telluride, Colorado, which goes up over a 13,000-foot-high ridge.

Though Bob works out long and hard each day, he knows that training like this is not for the average person. Through his travels, lectures, and workshops, he's kept in constant touch with people in all degrees of physical condition.

Jean Anderson, Bob's wife, plays a major role in the design and development of Stretching Inc.'s large line of stretching products *(see p. M-37)*. Jean was born in Long Beach, California, and is a graduate of California State University at Long Beach, where she received her B.A. in art. In the early '70s, when Bob was teaching stretching to the Denver Broncos, the Los Angeles Lakers, and the New York Jets, Jean developed a system of doing line drawings from photos of Bob doing the stretches. Jean also works with Bob in developing the stretching instructions and creating and producing their various stretching books, posters, and videotapes.

*including Chinese, Lithuanian and Slovenian

Credits

Editor
Lloyd Kahn

Contributing Editors
Stuart Kenter
Robert Lewandowski
George Young

Art Director
David Wills

Design
Rick Gordon
Lloyd Kahn

Design Consultant
Janet Bollow

Cover Design
David Wills

Production Manager
Rick Gordon

Production Assistant
Christina Reski

Proofreading & Indexing
Frances Bowles

Models for Drawings
Bob Anderson
Jean Anderson
Joan Creed
Linda Donahue
Bob Kahn
Kay Labella
Grace London
Christina Reski
Dave Roche
Vandy Seeburg
JoAnne Sercl
Peggy Sterling
Sandy Thomas
Joyce Werth

Special thanks to the following people, who helped with this book in one way or another:
Sally Carlson
Joan Creed
Page Dickinson
Michelle Donahue
Lesley Kahn
Paul Marxhausen
Maureen Watts

Production Hardware
Macintosh G4
Agfa Arcus II Scanner

Production Software
QuarkXpress®
Adobe Photoshop®
Adobe Illustrator®

Typefaces
Adobe Minion, Cosmos, Frutiger
Zapf Dingbats

Paper
60# Williamsburg Matte

Printing
Courier Companies, Inc., Westford, MA

StretchWare

by Bob Anderson
for Macintosh and Windows 95/98/ME/NT/2000/XP

The same machine that causes the problem now contains the solution!

StretchWare is a computer program based on this book, *Stretching in the Office*, and the User Manual for the program is included on the following pages.

StretchWare is software that reminds you to stretch at your computer. Every hour (or other designated time period), a window pops up on your screen, asking "Do you have time to stretch?" If you click OK, the stretches pop up on the screen.

When you roll your mouse over each stretch, the instructions appear in a small window.

You can also set StretchWare to go off at certain times of the day, or when you reach a certain number of keystrokes or mouse clicks.

StretchWare is a great reminder for you to take a few minutes during the day to stretch, helping you avoid the stiffness and soreness that come from constant sitting.

• To remind you: a chime and a flashing icon.

• To guide you: the stretches appear onscreen.

• To customize: set your own personal preferences.

STRETCH*WARE*™

THE SOFTWARE THAT REMINDS YOU
TO **S T R E T C H !**

by Bob Anderson

illustrated by Jean Anderson

design and watercolors
by Chelsea Sammel

For Macintosh
and Windows

The machine that
causes the problem
now contains
the solution!

Created by
Shelter Publications

USER
MANUAL

STRETCHWARE™ LICENSE AGREEMENT

PLEASE READ THIS AGREEMENT CAREFULLY
BEFORE INSTALLING THIS SOFTWARE.

By installing this software, you agree to the terms of this license (see below). If you do not agree to the terms of this license, do NOT use this software; return the CD-ROM in its unopened sleeve and your money will be refunded.

License and Permitted Use. StretchWare™ ("Software") is licensed, not sold, to you by Shelter Publications, Inc. ("Shelter"). Shelter grants you a nonexclusive license to:

    (a) Use one copy of Software at a time.
    (b) Install one copy of Software on the hard disk of one computer; this copy must contain the Shelter copyright notice.
    (c) Make one copy of Software disk for backup purposes; this copy must contain the Shelter copyright notice.

Restrictions. You may NOT use Software on more than one computer and you may NOT distribute copies of Software to others by any methods, including, but not limited to, electronic means, or via internet or intranet technology. Software contains trade secrets and to protect them you may NOT decompile, reverse engineer, merge, or disassemble software, or reduce software to a humanly perceivable form. You may not modify, adapt, translate, rent, loan, resell, distribute, network, or create any derivative work based upon software or any part thereof.

Medical Warning. The stretches and other information in Software are not meant to substitute for medical diagnosis and/or treatment. Consult your physician or health professional BEFORE trying any new physical activity. You hereby agree to read the instructions "How To Stretch" on pp. 8–9 of the User Manual and/or in the "Topics" window of Software before performing any of the stretches illustrated in Software.

Termination of License. The License is effective until terminated. The License will terminate immediately without notice if you fail to comply with any of its provisions. Upon termination, you agree to destroy Software.

Limited Warranty. As its only warranty under this agreement, Shelter warrants Software to be free of defects in materials under normal use for a period of 90 days from the date of the delivery to you, as evidenced by your purchase receipt.

Warranty Disclaimer. The above warranty is exclusive and in lieu of all other warranties, whether expressed or implied. No oral or written information or advice given by Shelter, its officers, employees, affiliates, distributors, dealers, sales representatives, or agents shall increase the scope of the above Limited Warranty or create any new warranties. SOFTWARE IS PROVIDED "AS IS," AND THE ENTIRE RISK AS TO THE QUALITY AND PERFORMANCE OF SOFTWARE IS WITH YOU. SHELTER DOES NOT WARRANT THAT SOFTWARE WILL MEET YOUR REQUIREMENTS, OR THAT THE FUNCTIONS CONTAINED IN THE SOFTWARE WILL BE UNINTERRUPTED OR ERROR-FREE, OR THAT SOFTWARE DEFECTS OR CONFLICTS WILL BE CORRECTED. IN NO EVENT WILL SHELTER OR ITS OFFICERS, EMPLOYEES, AFFILIATES, DISTRIBUTORS, DEALERS, SALES REPRESENTATIVES, OR AGENTS BE LIABLE TO YOU FOR ANY CONSEQUENTIAL, INCIDENTAL, OR INDIRECT DAMAGES (INCLUDING DAMAGES FOR LOSS OF BUSINESS PROFITS, BUSINESS INTERRUPTION, LOSS OF BUSINESS INFORMATION, AND THE LIKE) OR PERSONAL INJURY ARISING OUT OF THE USE OR INABILITY TO USE SOFTWARE OR ACCOMPANYING WRITTEN MATERIALS— EVEN IF SHELTER OR AN AUTHORIZED SHELTER REPRESENTATIVE HAS BEEN ADVISED OF THE POSSIBILITY OF SUCH DAMAGES.

    SOME JURISDICTIONS DO NOT ALLOW THE EXCLUSION OF IMPLIED WARRANTIES, SO THE ABOVE EXCLUSION MAY NOT APPLY.

    In no event shall Shelter's total liability to you for all damages, losses, and causes of action (whether in contract, tort, including negligence, or otherwise) exceed the amount paid for the software and its documentation.

Governing Law. This agreement is governed by the laws of the state of California.

SHELTER PUBLICATIONS, INC.
P. O. Box 279
Bolinas, CA 94924 U.S.A.

The human body was not designed
to sit for long periods of time.
Holding still for much of the day
is a recent phenomenon
in human history.

The object of StretchWare™ is to keep
your body—joints, muscles, and
circulation—healthy and fit even
though you may sit and/or work
at a computer much of the day.

CD-ROM Contents

In addition to the installers, the StretchWare™ CD-ROM contains the following items:

1. A Read me file containing installation instructions.
2. A copy of this user manual in Adobe Acrobat PDF format (Adobe Acrobat Reader installer included).
3. The Shelter Publications catalog in Adobe Acrobat PDF format, containing double-clickable links to Shelter's website.
4. Double-clickable link icons to open your web browser to Shelter's website or the StretchWare™ home page.
5. Installer components organized to fit on floppy disks *(Windows only)*.

Windows users: If AutoLaunch is enabled on your computer, the installer will start to run when you insert the StretchWare™ CD-ROM (unless you hold down the shift key when you put the disc in). You can quit from the installer by choosing **No** when the license agreement window comes up. You can then right-click on the CD-ROM icon in **My Computer** and choose **Explore**. The items listed above will be found in the various folders on the CD-ROM.

Medical Advisory

The stretches and other information in StretchWare™ are not meant to substitute for medical diagnosis and/or treatment. Do not try any of the stretches if you have an existing physical problem. Consult your physician or health professional BEFORE trying any new physical activity. Please read the instructions "How to Stretch" on pp. 8–9 of this manual and/or in the **Topics** window of StretchWare™ before performing any of the stretches illustrated in StretchWare™.

StretchWare™ is the trademark of Shelter Publications, Inc.

Contents

1 Introduction

Congratulations on licensing StretchWare™, the software that reminds you to stretch. You can make it a useful tool in caring for your body while you work at a computer.

> **The same machine that causes the problem now contains the solution!**

Taking regular stretching breaks will help you to avoid repetitive-strain injuries such as carpal tunnel syndrome. Stretch breaks can also improve your circulation, counteract stiffness, and simply make you feel better.

StretchWare™ has been carefully designed to:

- be simple and intuitive.
- offer a wide range of options as to when and how to use it.
- work seamlessly with other software.

Please follow the installation instructions on pp. 4 and 5. You will be on your way to safer and more comfortable computing. And remember, we have designed StretchWare™ so that it could be tailored to your needs. Don't hesitate to change things around until you find the right combination for yourself.

To your very good health!

P. S. Remember to exercise too, whenever you can — take a walk, climb some stairs, ride a bike. It all helps when you spend hours sitting.

Why StretchWare™?

Today's workplace is fast-paced and demanding. Daily use of computers has led to new levels of stress and repetitive strain injuries (RSIs)—which have increased by 80% in the last decade. According to the U.S. Bureau of Labor Statistics, RSIs are now the single largest category of workplace-related injuries. Shoulder tension, lower back pain, and wrist problems, such as carpal tunnel syndrome, now affect millions of Americans.

Though exact figures are hard to pin down, it is widely accepted that computer-related RSIs cost U.S. businesses billions of dollars in medical claims and lost productivity every year. These injuries include carpal tunnel syndrome, tendinitis, shoulder and neck pain, and others. A recent report published in *USA Today* put the yearly cost of RSIs to American employers at over $100 billion a year.

According to the National Council of Compensation Insurance, the average compensation awarded to a victim of carpal tunnel syndrome is $33,000.

It may seem hard to believe that simple stretches can do so much to overcome these problems, but it's true. Stretching can help prevent problems like carpal tunnel syndrome before they occur, and in many cases, help rehabilitate existing conditions.

What Is StretchWare™?

StretchWare™ is a program that reminds you to stretch at your computer. Once installed, it remains dormant in the background until it is time for a break.

You can configure StretchWare™ to your own particular needs and work schedule. A typical configuration has a chime sound and a small flashing icon to notify you when it is time for a stretching break. If you want a more noticeable reminder, you can have a window appear mid-screen asking if you have time to stretch.

If you choose to stretch at that time, a stretching routine of your choice then appears on the screen. (The stretches will never interrupt you when you are busy—you have to call for them.)

2 Installation

Note: By installing this software, you agree to the terms of the License Agreement appearing (on page i) in the front of this manual.

Macintosh

System Requirements

- System 7.0 or later, OS X in Classic mode
- Works with 68K or PowerPC processors
- Color or grayscale monitor 640 × 480 or larger
  (1-bit black-and-white monitors not supported)

Instructions

1. Insert the installation CD-ROM.

2. Double-click on the StretchWare™ Installer icon and follow the on-screen instructions.

NO CD-ROM DRIVE?

1. Locate another computer with a CD-ROM drive and copy the StretchWare™ Installer onto a floppy disk, which you can then use to install.

2. Double-click on the StretchWare™ Installer icon and follow the on-screen instructions.

UNINSTALLING STRETCHWARE™

If, for one reason or another, you want to remove StretchWare™ altogether, remove StretchWare™ from the Extensions folder (inside the System Folder) or disable it with the Extensions Manager.

Windows

System Requirements

- Windows 95/98/ME/NT/2000/XP
- Color or grayscale monitor 640 × 480 or larger
  (1-bit black-and-white monitors not supported)

Instructions

INSTALLING FROM THE CD-ROM

Insert the installation CD-ROM. If AutoLaunch is supported on your computer, the installation will proceed automatically; otherwise, continue with the following instructions.

1. Double-click on **My Computer** on the Desktop, which will open the main browsing window.
2. Double-click on the CD-ROM icon named **Stretch**, which will show you the contents of the CD-ROM.
3. Double-click on **Install,** which will open the window for the **Install** folder.
4. Double-click the **Setup** application. This may be named **Setup.exe**, depending on your computer's configuration.
5. The installer will run.
6. If you have installed over a previous version of StretchWare™, restart your computer to ensure that all components of the earlier version have been removed.

Note for Windows NT, 2000, or XP installation: You must first be logged in with Administrative Rights before installing.

The CD-ROM also contains disk images for installing from a floppy disk, copies of the StretchWare™ Manual and Shelter Catalog in Adobe Acrobat PDF format, an Adobe Acrobat Reader installer, and links to Shelter's website.

NO CD-ROM DRIVE? TO MAKE INSTALLER FLOPPY DISKS

1. Locate another computer with a CD-ROM drive, insert the CD-ROM, and open the "Diskettes" folder on the CD-ROM. *(For information on accessing any of the folders on the CD-ROM, see the bottom of this page.)*

2. Open the folder named Disk 1 and copy its contents to one floppy disk.

3. Open the folder named Disk 2 and copy its contents to a second floppy disk.

INSTALLING FROM FLOPPY DISKS

1. Go to the **Start** button, select **Settings**, click on **Control Panel** and double-click on **Add/Remove Programs**.

2. From under the Install/Uninstall tab (which should be active by default), click the **Install...** button.

3. You will be prompted to insert the first installation floppy disk. Afterwards, you will be prompted to insert the second installation floppy disk.

4. If you have installed over a previous version of StretchWare™, restart your computer to ensure that all components of the earlier version have been removed.

UNINSTALLING STRETCHWARE™

If, for any reason, you want to remove StretchWare™ altogether, here's how to do it:

1. Go to the **Start** button, select **Settings**, click on **Control Panel** and double-click on **Add/Remove Programs**.

2. From under the Install/Uninstall tab (which should be active by default), choose StretchWare™ from the list of programs and click the **Add/Remove...** button.

3. When the uninstall is complete, click the **OK** button.

4. Restart your computer.

ACCESSING FOLDERS ON THE CD-ROM

1. Insert the CD-ROM while holding down the shift key to bypass AutoLaunch.

2. Double-click on **My Computer** on the Desktop, which will open the main browsing window.

3. Right-click on the CD-ROM icon named **Stretch**, and choose **Explore**, which will show you the contents of the CD-ROM.

3 The Basics

How StretchWare™ Works

The Stretching Reminder

You will be reminded to stretch periodically by:

- a sound of your choice
- a flashing icon
- and/or a dialog box

You can choose any, all, or none of these methods.

None of these will interfere with the program(s) you are currently running.

Customizing

You will be able to tailor the program to your personal needs by setting the preferences.

The Reminder

Periodically, a chime will sound and/or an icon will flash, to remind you it's time to stretch.

The Stretching Routines

A stretching routine will then appear on-screen to guide you through a series of stretches.

The Topics

Information on stretching, repetitive strain injuries, ergonomics, and other useful information is presented under the **Topics** pull-down menu.

How to Stretch

The Right Way to Stretch

- Breathe easily.
- Relax.
- Tune into your body.
- Focus on muscles and joints being stretched.
- Feel the stretch.
- Be guided by the *feel* of the stretch.
- No bouncing!
- No pain!

The Wrong Way to Stretch

- Holding your breath
- Being in a hurry
- Not being focused on your body
- Stretching while tense
- Bouncing
- Stretching to the point of pain

Two Phases

There are two phases to each stretch: the easy stretch and the developmental stretch. They are done one after the other.

The Easy Stretch

Stretch until you feel a mild tension, and hold for 5 to 10 seconds. Relax. As you hold the stretch, the feeling of tension should diminish. If it doesn't, ease off slightly into a more comfortable stretch. The easy stretch maintains flexibility, loosens muscles and tight tendons, and reduces muscle tension.

The Developmental Stretch

Now, move a fraction of an inch farther into the stretch, until you feel mild tension again. Hold for 5 to 10 seconds. Again, the feeling should diminish or stay the same. If the tension increases or becomes painful, you are overstretching—back off into a more comfortable stretch. The developmental stretch further reduces tension and increases flexibility.

Points to Keep in Mind

- Always stretch within the limits of what is comfortable for you, never stretch to the point of pain.
- Breathe slowly, rhythmically, and with control. Do not hold your breath.
- Take your time. A long, mild stretch reduces unwanted muscle tension and tightness.
- Do not compare yourself with others. We are all different. Comparisons may lead to overstretching.
- If you are stretching correctly, the mild tension should subside slightly as you hold the stretch.
- Any stretch that grows in intensity or becomes painful indicates you are overstretching—the drastic stretch.

Pay attention to how each stretch feels.

Hold only stretch tensions that feel good. Relax while you concentrate on the area being stretched.

How far should I stretch?

Your body is different every day. Be guided by how the stretch feels.

Stretching is not exercise!

You are stretching, not exercising. You don't need to push it. Stretching is a mild, gentle activity.

Give it 2 to 3 weeks for benefits.

The benefits come from regularity. Stick with it and see how you feel in a few weeks.

Meet the Flashing Icon

Macintosh Users

Because they are so important in using StretchWare™, we'd like to explain how the icons function.

The StretchWare™ flashing icon, which brings up the special menu

The StretchWare™ application icon, which shows when StretchWare™ is the active application

On the Macintosh, the flashing icon appears toward the right side of the menu bar, and to the left of the active application icon. This icon is the "station central" for StretchWare™. It will flash when the reminder goes off. It will also serve the following functions:

1. If you double-click on the icon, it will bring up the next stretching routine on-screen. (With System 7, click on the icon.)

2. If you click and hold on the icon, a pull-down menu appears. You can then choose one of the following:

   • Stretch now.

   • Don't stretch now.

   • Delay stretch by 5. 10, or 15 minutes.

   • Select a stretching routine.

   • Call up the preferences.

Try it:

   • Click on the icon with your mouse.

   • Look at the pull-down menu.

   • Try the different alternatives. See how they work.

   • Double-click on the icon to see how it brings up a stretching routine. (With System 7, click on the icon.)

The *application icon* (the clock) appears at the extreme right side of the menu bar when StretchWare™ is the active (frontmost) application.

Meet the Flashing Icon

Windows Users

Because it is so important in using StretchWare™, we'd like to explain how the icon functions.

In Windows, the flashing icon appears in the Task Tray (the portion of the Taskbar near the digital clock readout). This icon is the "station central" for StretchWare™. It will flash when the reminder goes off. It will also serve the following functions:

1. If you double-click on the icon, it will bring up the next stretching routine on-screen.

2. If you right-click on the icon, a pop-up menu appears. You can then choose one of the following:

   - Stretch now.
   - Don't stretch now.
   - Delay stretch by 5. 10, or 15 minutes.
   - Select a stretching routine.
   - Call up the preferences.

Try it:

   - Right-click on the icon with your mouse.
   - Look at the pull-down menu.
   - Try the different alternatives. See how they work.
   - Double-click on the icon to see how it brings up a stretching routine.

StretchWare™ Menus

Here are four pull-down menus that appear only when StretchWare™ is open and in front of all other applications.

Windows

Macintosh

Both Windows and Macintosh

Stretches

- Adios (Shutdown) Stretches
- Before-Walking Stretches
- ✓ Good Morning! (Startup) Stretches
- Graphic Artist Stretches
- Hand, Arm, Shoulder & Neck Stretches
- Hand, Wrist & Forearm Stretches
- Keyboard Operator Stretches
- Lower Back Stretches
- Neck & Shoulder Stiffness
- Online Stretches
- On-the-Phone Stretches
- Spontaneous Stretches
- Standing Stretches
- Stressed-Out Stretches

Topics

- ✓ Welcome to StretchWare™
- Getting Started — Right Now!
- Introduction
- Computer & Desk Problems
- Benefits of Stretching
- When & Where to Stretch
- How to Stretch
- Repetitive Strain Injuries
- Ergonomic Principles
- Online Resources
- Shelter Fitness Resources

The StretchWare™ Main Menu

Windows: The StretchWare™ main menu can be accessed by right-clicking on the StretchWare™ icon in the Task Tray (the portion of the Taskbar near the digital clock readout).

Macintosh: The StretchWare™ main menu can be accessed by clicking and dragging on the StretchWare™ icon (near the right side of the menu bar).

This menu can be activated at any time, since the icon is always present. It doesn't matter what program you are in—you can always use the icon menu to activate a stretching routine or to open the preferences.

Stretch Now
Don't Stretch Now
Delay Stretching 5 Minutes
Delay Stretching 10 Minutes
Delay Stretching 15 Minutes
Adios (Shutdown) Stretches
Before-Walking Stretches
Good Morning! (Startup) Stretches
Graphic Artist Stretches
Hand, Arm, Shoulder & Neck Stretches
Hand, Wrist & Forearm Stretches
Keyboard Operator Stretches
Lower Back Stretches
Neck & Shoulder Stiffness
Online Stretches
On-the-Phone Stretches
Spontaneous Stretches
Standing Stretches
Stressed-Out Stretches
Preferences...

> Think of all the times you have felt stiff or sore and stretching could have helped. Spend a few minutes now seeing how the program works.

4 Preferences

StretchWare™ has been designed so you can tailor it to your needs. You can choose how often the reminders appear, and the methods used to remind you. According to your needs and work schedule, you can set up StretchWare™ to be as unobtrusive or as persistent as you like.

This is what the Preferences window looks like. You can open it at any time by going to the stretching icon, or by going to **Edit** in the menu bar when StretchWare™ is open.

The four tabs you will see are:

- **How to Activate** • **How to Notify** • **Sequence of Routines** • **Hot Key**

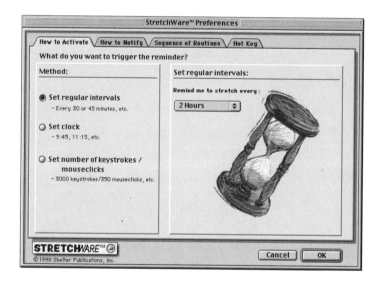

Click on any of the four tabs to bring different preferences to the front.

The settings are simple, and making choices is easy and intuitive. Before you set the preferences, click on the different tabs and watch what appears on-screen.

The different preferences windows are shown on pages 15 through 23.

M-14

Preferences: How to Activate

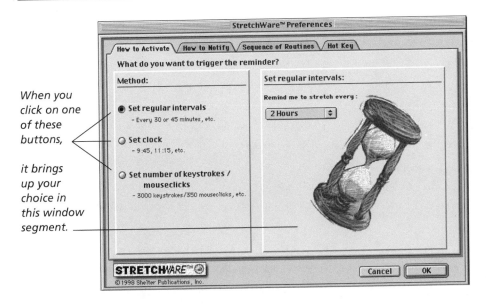

When you click on one of these buttons,

it brings up your choice in this window segment.

Choose how to activate the reminder. In other words, what should prompt the computer to remind you to stretch?

Here are the options:

1. **Set regular intervals**
   Every 30 minutes, 45 minutes, 2 hours, etc.

2. **Set clock**
   You choose specific times of the day when you want to be reminded (that is, 9:15 A.M., 10:30 A.M., 1:15 A.M., etc.)

3. **Set number of keystrokes/mouse clicks (whichever comes first)**
   After a certain number of mouse clicks or keystrokes, the reminder is activated. You can choose from the suggested allotments or set your own.

Pages 16, 17, and 18 show you explain each of the activation methods.

Preferences: How to Activate

1. SET REGULAR INTERVALS OF TIME

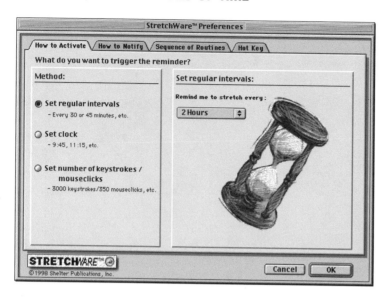

This is a very simple method. The reminder goes off at regular intervals: every 45 minutes, 60 minutes, 75 minutes, etc.

If the reminder comes up when you are busy and you don't want to be interrupted, you can choose not to stretch or delay the reminder 5, 10, or 15 minutes.

> ## Default Settings
>
> By default, StretchWare™ is preset to have the sound of a Tibetan bell go off every hour, with a flashing icon for a visual reminder. This setup is very simple. You may want to leave these settings until you get used to the program and then later set your own preferences.

Preferences: How to Activate

2. SET CLOCK FOR SPECIFIC TIMES OF DAY

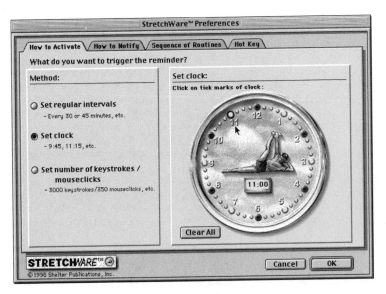

This is the interactive StretchWare™ clock. Here you set specific times during the day—*in 15-minute increments*—by clicking your mouse directly on the clock's number buttons.

For example, you may want to set it for the time you get to work so that you can start the day by loosening up, or set it for 15 minutes before lunch, or just before you quit for the day, etc.

Here's what the buttons look like:

- On a color monitor, unselected buttons are gold; selected buttons are red with a black center.
- On a grayscale monitor, unselected buttons are light gray; selected buttons are dark gray with a black center.

When your mouse rolls over a button, the time appears in the digital window on the face of the clock. If you make a mistake or want to change the chosen times, simply depress an active (red) button on the clock and it will become unselected—or click the **Clear All** button.

Preferences: How to Activate

3. SELECT NUMBER OF KEYSTROKES/MOUSECLICKS

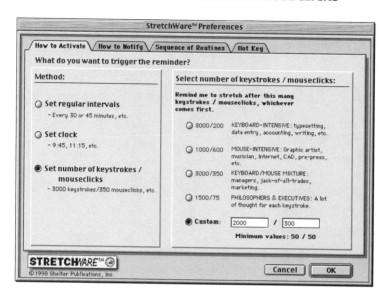

Depending on how you use your computer, you may find this method useful since it measures your actual keyboard and mouse usage. Whether you do steady data entry, typesetting, graphics work, or use the web—you can choose the threshold when you want a stretching reminder.

The reminder will be activated when either the keystroke or mouseclick number is reached—*whichever comes first.*

Some samples of keyboard/mouseclick combinations are given, according to type of work performed. These are only starting points; you will have to experiment with different settings—adjusting the intervals to your own work habits. Everyone is different! You can choose a custom setting and set the number of keystrokes or mouseclicks to any value from 50 to 999,999.

> These settings are very easy to change. Change them as often as you need for normal days, or to relieve a problem when it occurs. The formula is in your hands!

Preferences: How to Notify

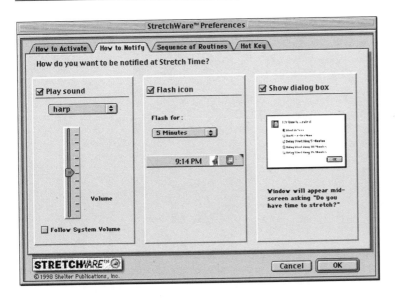

Now that you've selected a method of activation, let's determine *how* you want to be notified.

StretchWare™ offers one audio, and two visual methods. You can choose one, two, or all three options. Options are selected by clicking in the checkboxes. At least one box must be checked for notification to occur. The options are as follows:

1. **Play sound** will cause a sound of your choice to play, at a volume you choose.

2. **Flash icon** will show the figure in the taskbar *(Windows)* or the menu bar *(Macintosh)* moving through stretches, and continue for as long as you choose.

3. **Show dialog box** will have pop-up window appear with the message, "Do you have time to stretch?" You can then choose one of the following options:

   - **Stretch now**
   - **Don't stretch now**
   - **Delay stretching 5 minutes**
   - **Delay stretching 10 minutes**
   - **Delay stretching 15 minutes**

M-19

Preferences: Sequence of Routines

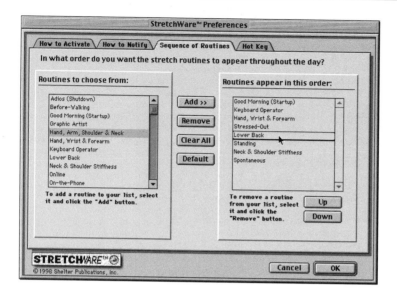

The box at the left shows the 14 stretching routines. The box at the right displays the order in which the routines will appear throughout the day.

To set up your own sequence, follow these steps:

- Click on a routine in the left box.
- While holding down the mouse, drag your selected routine to the right box.
- Release the mouse to drop it into place.
  (See page 21 if your computer does not have the Drag and Drop option.)
  or:
- Highlight a routine in the left box by clicking on it. Then click the **Add** button. The routine will appear in the right box.

The four buttons in the middle have the following functions:

- **Remove** will delete a routine.
- **Clear All** will delete the routines in the right box. (Great for starting over.)
- **Default** will select our preset order of eight stretching routines.

No Drag and Drop Option?

If you do not have the Drag and Drop option, changing the order of your sequence is accomplished as follows:

1. Click on a routine to select it.

2. Click the **Up** or **Down** buttons to move it around.

Note: On the Macintosh, Drag and Drop is included with System 7.5 and higher. The Drag and Drop extension is available from Apple's website for systems 7.1.2 and higher. If your computer does not support Drag and Drop, you can still use the **Add**, **Remove**, **Up**, and **Down** buttons as described on the previous page.

Your customized sequence of routines will apply when you:

   (a) double-click on the StretchWare™ icon (click in System 7)

   (b) select **Stretch Now** from the StretchWare™ icon menu

   (c) select **Stretch Now** from the reminder window when it appears

   (d) press the Hot Key combination

But what happens if you decide to stretch without the reminder? Say you feel the need to stretch and select a stretching routine from either the icon or the **Stretches** menu—on your own volition.

The predetermined sequence will *not* be affected. The next time you perform any one of the actions, (a), (b), (c), or (d) above, the next stretch in the chosen sequence will appear, just as if you had not chosen a routine in between.

Variety Is the Spice . . .

Change the sequence of routines to suit your daily needs. If you have neck stiffness, for example, you may want to set it so that every other stretch break is *Neck & Shoulder Stretches.*

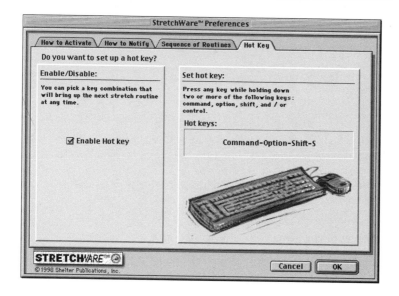

Hot key refers to a combination of keys depressed at the same time to trigger an action. How can you use it with StretchWare™?

You may feel the need to stretch between reminders. Or, you may not want any reminders and choose to stretch only when you feel like it. In either case, you can use a hot key to bring up a stretching routine.

The default hot key combination is *command-option-shift-S*—already set.

Or you can create a combination of your own. To do this, open the **Hot Key** tab in the Preferences window and press the keys of your choice—all at the same time. You must include two or more of these keys: *command, option, shift,* or *control* along with one additional key. Your selection will appear in the box.

Note: The only combination that doesn't work here is *option-shift,* which is often required to type certain special characters.

So, whenever you have a small window of opportunity to stretch, or just feel tense, hit the hot key and stretch that tension away!

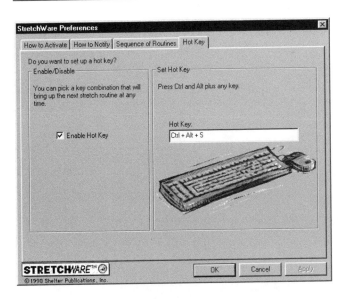

Hot key refers to a combination of keys depressed at the same time to trigger an action. How can you use it with StretchWare™?

You may feel the need to stretch between reminders. Or, you may not want any reminders and choose to stretch only when you feel like it. In either case, you can use a hot key to bring up a stretching routine.

The default hot key combination is *Ctrl-Alt-S*—already set.

Or you can alter the combination to include a key of your choice. To do this, click on the **Hot Key** tab in the Preferences window. The cursor is already active in the Hot Key window. Depress *Ctrl-Alt* or *Ctrl-Shift-Alt* and any other key of your choosing. Your selection will appear in the box.

So, whenever you have a small window of opportunity to stretch, or just feel tense, hit the hot key and stretch that tension away!

5 Stretching Routines

Here is one of the 14 stretching routines available in StretchWare™:

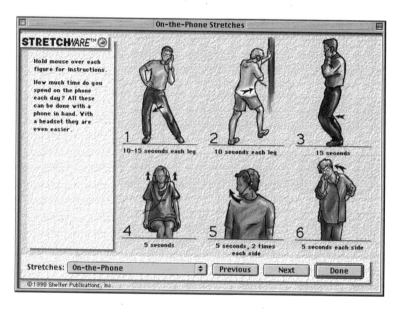

To see all 14 available routines
Macintosh: Click and hold on the StretchWare™ icon.
Windows: Right-click on the StretchWare™ icon.

To activate a routine of your choice
Select the routine with your mouse; the routine will appear on-screen.

To go to the previous or next routine
Click the **Previous** or **Next** buttons at the bottom of the window.

To close the stretching window

Macintosh: Click the **Done** button (leaving StretchWare™ open in the background) or click on **Quit** in the **File** menu *(Command-Q)* to quit StretchWare™.

Windows: Click the **Exit** button or choose **Exit** from the **File** menu *(Alt-F-X)*.

To quickly bring the next scheduled routine on-screen

Macintosh: Double-click on the icon. (With System 7, click on the icon.)

Windows: Double-click on the icon.

Here is another routine, showing the pop-up instructions:

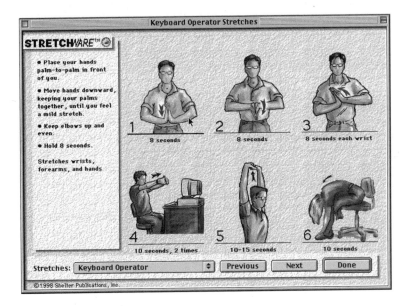

Instructions for each stretch will pop up on-screen when you roll your mouse over that stretch. Try it!

> **After you follow the instructions a few times,**
> **you'll be able to stretch by just looking at the drawings.**

6 Topics

Information on stretching, repetitive strain injuries, ergonomics, and other computer and/or office-related health issues are presented under **Topics** in the menu bar. Click on it with with your mouse to see the available topics.

Important: Please read *How to Stretch* before you start stretching.

Time well spent: Read through the other topics as well. They are highly condensed (for busy people) and contain up-to-date information on avoiding repetitive strain injuries, tips on ergonomics, and advice on what to do if you are already injured. There is also a valuable reference section to the latest books and online information for more extensive information on any of these subjects.

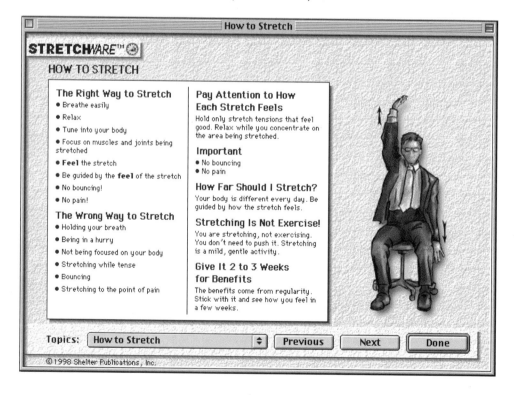

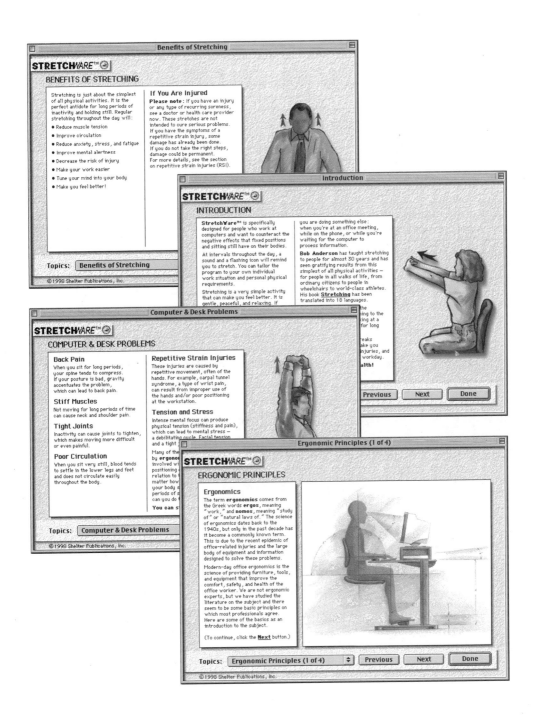

Benefits of Stretching

STRETCH*WARE*™

BENEFITS OF STRETCHING

Stretching is just about the simplest of all physical activities. It is the perfect antidote for long periods of inactivity and holding still. Regular stretching throughout the day will:

- Reduce muscle tension
- Improve circulation
- Reduce anxiety, stress, and fatigue
- Improve mental alertness
- Decrease the risk of injury
- Make your work easier
- Tune your mind into your body
- Make you feel better!

If You Are Injured

Please note: If you have an injury or any type of recurring soreness, see a doctor or health care provider now. These stretches are not intended to cure serious problems. If you have the symptoms of a repetitive strain injury, some damage has already been done. If you do not take the right steps, damage could be permanent. For more details, see the section on repetitive strain injuries (RSI).

Topics: **Benefits of Stretching**

©1998 Shelter Publications, Inc.

Introduction

STRETCH*WARE*™

INTRODUCTION

StretchWare™ is specifically designed for people who work at computers and want to counteract the negative effects that fixed positions and sitting still have on their bodies.

At intervals throughout the day, a sound and a flashing icon will remind you to stretch. You can tailor the program to your own individual work situation and personal physical requirements.

Stretching is a very simple activity that can make you feel better. It is gentle, peaceful, and relaxing. If you are doing something else: when you're at an office meeting, while on the phone, or while you're waiting for the computer to process information.

Bob Anderson has taught stretching to people for almost 30 years and has seen gratifying results from this simplest of all physical activities — for people in all walks of life, from ordinary citizens to people in wheelchairs to world-class athletes. His book **Stretching** has been translated in 18 languages.

Previous | Next | Done

Computer & Desk Problems

STRETCH*WARE*™

COMPUTER & DESK PROBLEMS

Back Pain
When you sit for long periods, your spine tends to compress. If your posture is bad, gravity accentuates the problem, which can lead to back pain.

Stiff Muscles
Not moving for long periods of time can cause neck and shoulder pain.

Tight Joints
Inactivity can cause joints to tighten, which makes moving more difficult or even painful.

Poor Circulation
When you sit very still, blood tends to settle in the lower legs and feet and does not circulate easily throughout the body.

Repetitive Strain Injuries
These injuries are caused by repetitive movement, often of the hands. For example, carpal tunnel syndrome, a type of wrist pain, can result from improper use of the hands and/or poor positioning at the workstation.

Tension and Stress
Intense mental focus can produce physical tension (stiffness and pain), which can lead to mental stress — a debilitating cycle. Facial tension and a tight

Many of the
by **ergonom**
involved wi
positioning o
relation to
matter how
your body s
periods of s
can you do t

You can st

Topics: **Computer & Desk Problems**

©1998 Shelter Publications, Inc.

Ergonomic Principles (1 of 4)

STRETCH*WARE*™

ERGONOMIC PRINCIPLES

Ergonomics
The term **ergonomics** comes from the Greek words **ergos**, meaning "work," and **nomos**, meaning "study of" or "natural laws of." The science of ergonomics dates back to the 1940s, but only in the past decade has it become a commonly known term. This is due to the recent epidemic of office-related injuries and the large body of equipment and information designed to solve these problems.

Modern-day office ergonomics is the science of providing furniture, tools, and equipment that improve the comfort, safety, and health of the office worker. We are not ergonomic experts, but we have studied the literature on the subject and there seem to be some basic principles on which most professionals agree. Here are some of the basics as an introduction to the subject.

(To continue, click the **Next** button.)

Topics: **Ergonomic Principles (1 of 4)** ◆ | Previous | Next | Done

©1998 Shelter Publications, Inc.

7 Tips and Tricks

Here are some tips, tricks, and shortcuts. These are from folks who have used the program for a while and have discovered quick ways to achieve various results.

Turning off the reminder

Go to **Preferences...**, click on the **How to Notify** tab, and uncheck each of the three boxes (**Play sound**, **Flash icon**, and **Display dialog box**). When you get the warning dialog, click **OK**.

The easiest way to bring up a stretching routine

Double-clicking on the stretching icon will do the trick. With System 7 on the Macintosh, only a single click is needed.

If you are away from your computer when the reminder goes off

The icon will be flashing when you return (unless you have unclicked the box in preferences). Even if you have chosen for it to flash for, say, 5 minutes, it will not start the countdown until the first keystroke or mouseclick.

If you're in a real hurry, but still want to stretch

Let the stretching routine come up and go through the stretches very fast. Take maybe 10 to 15 seconds to do all the stretches. Then back to work. A little is better than nothing!

Where do you want the StretchWare™ windows to appear on-screen?

You can move the StretchWare™ window to any part of your screen, and it will continue to appear there. You might put it at the least-used part of your screen, perhaps the lower right.

If you have two monitors

Put the StretchWare™ window on the secondary monitor. This way you can allow it to come up and stay visible while you finish what you're doing.

You don't even have to stretch!

Use the bell and flashing icon to remind you to take a break. Do something for your body for a few seconds or minutes. Walk around. Think of your posture. Are you stiff or sore anywhere?

A tip on sound volume

Take a look at **How to Activate** in the Preferences window. On the left are the sound controls. At the bottom is a checkbox saying **Follow System Volume**. If this is clicked, the sound level you set in your computer's Sound Control Panel will govern the sound volume of the stretching reminder. This is handy if you want to lower the sound level of every thing temporarily (say on an airplane) so as not to disturb others. If you turn *off* the checkbox in **Follow System Volume**, then you can set a fixed volume using the slider above this checkbox.

Choosing a different stretching routine

If you have chosen to have the reminder window pop up when it's time to stretch, you can still select which stretching routine will appear at that time (rather than the next one in the preset sequence). Rather than using the radio buttons or **OK** button in the window, make your selection from the menu under the stretching icon.

Keyboard shortcuts

To go from one routine to another, or from one topic to the next:

Windows: Use the tab, spacebar, and arrow keys (either ← / → or ↑/↓) to cycle through the routines or topics.

Macintosh: Use the arrow keys (either ← / → or ↑/↓) to cycle through the routines or topics.

No notification

You can turn off all three methods of notification. This way, you will stretch only when you think of it by double-clicking on the stretching icon in the menu bar (single-clicking in Macintosh System 7), or by using the hot key. Go to the **How to Notify** tab in the Preferences window and deselect all three checkmarks.

Choosing a different stretching routine

If you have chosen to have the reminder window pop up when you want to be notified, you can still select the stretching routine that will appear at that time (rather than the next one in the preset sequence). Instead of using the radio buttons or the **OK** button in the reminder window, make your selection from the StretchWare™ main menu by clicking and holding on the stretching icon.

Ignoring keystrokes or mouseclicks

If you have chosen the **Set number of keystrokes/mouseclicks** option for the **How to Activate** tab in the Preferences window, you can choose to ignore either keystrokes or mouseclicks by choosing the **Custom** setting and putting in an extremely high number. A good choice would be 999,999 since this is the highest number that will be accepted by the program. Remember though: if you set both keystrokes *and* mouseclicks to such a high value, you will never get the stretching reminder.

Get buffed in the office.

"I set the program to go off 3 times a day, at 10, 2, and 4. I keep a pair of 20-pound dumbbells by my desk. For a month now, I've either been stretching or lifting weights 3 times a day. I feel more flexible and definitely better toned."

–Michael Rafferty, Bolinas, Calif.

You can do a lot with a pair of dumbbells. Try 3, 5, 10, 20 pounds—whatever will slightly stress the muscles with, say, 10 repetitions of most exercises. For other exercise ideas, point your web browser to *http://www.shelterpub.com/_fitness/ _weight_training/dumbell_training.html* for 16 different dumbbell exercises by Bill Pearl. Print them out and keep them in a desk drawer for easy reference.

8 FAQs

Frequently Asked Questions

Will StretchWare™ use much memory?

StretchWare™ has been carefully designed to use very little memory (1024K).

Will StretchWare™ interfere with running programs?

StretchWare™ runs behind the scenes. The stretching routines do not appear unless you activate them.

Why does StretchWare™ sometimes pop up right after a new time has been set in the preferences?

Since there are so many possible ways that you can choose to set up StretchWare™, the program does not restart the timing mechanism when the preferences are closed. Thus, when you shorten the notification time, the first reminder may seem premature. Don't worry—from that time on, it will work according to your choice.

Contacting Technical Support

Contact Technical Support at **support@shelterpub.com** .

9 Troubleshooting

StretchWare™ is compatible with PCs running Windows 95/98/ME/NT/2000/XP, as well as Apple Macintosh and Macintosh-compatible computers running System 7.0 or later. StretchWare™ is compatible with OS X in Classic mode.

*Contact Technical Support at **support@shelterpub.com**.*

StretchWare™ cannot be found, even after installation.

The StretchWare™ installer installs StretchWare™ onto your boot drive (system startup disk). If you are booting up from a different drive, StretchWare™ should be installed on that drive.

StretchWare™ remains open after clicking the **Done** button or closing the window *(Macintosh)*.

To save time on loading the program, StretchWare™ stays running after closing the stretching routine or topics windows. If you wish to free the memory used by StretchWare™ (only 1000 K), simply choose **Quit** under the **File** menu (or press *command-Q*) when you are done.

The hot key cannot be changed.

This often occurs when users have not selected a key combination that includes *at least two* of the modifier keys along with one character key.

Macintosh: Any combination of two or more of the following (along with one character key) is permissible: *command, option, shift, control*—except for *option-shift,* which is reserved for typing special characters. Special sequences reserved by the operating system, such as *command-option-escape* are not permitted.

Windows: Combinations of *Ctrl-Alt* and *Ctrl-Alt-Shift* along with one character key are permissible.

Two StretchWare™ icons show in the taskbar. *(Windows)*

After a reinstallation of StretchWare™, a second icon may appear in the taskbar. The extra icon will disappear either the next time the mouse is placed over the taskbar or after the computer is restarted.

Sometimes StretchWare™ notification does not work on time.

Occasionally, StretchWare's notification will be delayed. StretchWare™ is not able to safely interrupt on a few processor-intensive programs that shut off your computer's background functions (mostly video games). StretchWare™ will notify you that it is time to stretch the next time there is a pause, or when you return to the desktop. StretchWare™ is also designed so that it will not interrupt you while you are typing rapidly, but will wait for a pause.

StretchWare™ isn't making any notification sound.

If you are not hearing any sound when the stretch alert goes off, open the preferences, and under the **How to Notify** tab, make sure **Play sound** is selected. If **Play sound** is selected and you are still not hearing anything, close the window and open the appropriate control panel (**Sounds** on Windows — **Sound** or **Monitors & Sound** on the Macintosh). Make sure that your system sound is working, and that you can hear it. If you have external speakers, make sure they are connected and turned on. If your system sound is not working, you may need to reinstall your sound driver *(Windows)* or make sure that your sound card is properly configured.

The notification sound is either too quiet, too loud, or not following the system sound level.

The volume of the StretchWare™ notification sound may be set in the preferences under the **How to Notify** tab. If you wish notification volume to follow your system volume, select the **Follow System Volume** checkbox.

An incorrect stretching description is displayed when the stretching routine window is opened.

A description will come up in the left-hand portion of the window for whichever stretch the mouse is currently over. (The text by that stretch, containing the sequence number and the suggested repetitions, will change from blue to red.) Simply move the mouse over the stretch you want to do in order to get the relevant instructions. If the mouse is not positioned over any stretch, a general description related to the routine will be displayed.

Installation fails with "error 132." *(Windows XP)*

If another user is logged in and using StretchWare™ when you run the installer, you will get "error 132." This error appears because StretchWare™ is in use and cannot be updated. If you get the "error 132" message, have all users log off the machine before installing. This is only an issue with Windows XP.

Index of Stretches

Here is a unique feature of StretchWare™ that originated from Bob Anderson's classic book, *Stretching*. All the stretches in the program are summarized here. This index can be used in two ways:

- Make up your own routines by choosing combinations of stretches. You can do this after you have been using the routines for a while.
- If you have an RSI injury or anything you suspect could be a problem, print out these two pages so your doctor or health care professional can circle stretches recommended for your individual physical problem(s).

Hands & Wrists

Shoulders & Arms

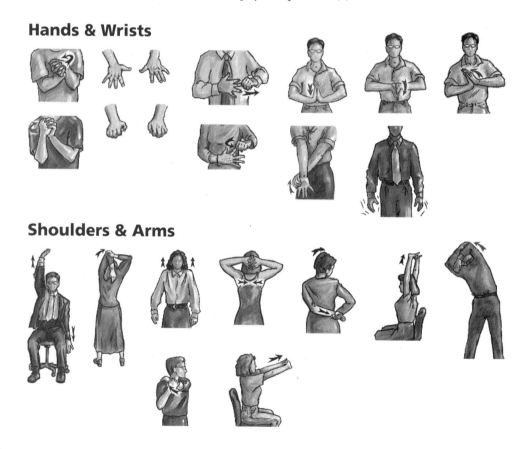

Neck & Shoulders

Chest

Legs

Back

More World-Class Fitness Books from Shelter Publications

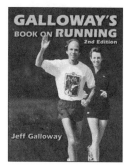

Galloway's Book on Running
2nd Edition
by Jeff Galloway

A complete revision of Olympian Jeff Galloway's classic book on running.

- 430,000 copies of original edition sold
- Training programs for 5K, 10K, and half-marathons
- The second running boom
- New info on diet, "slow" running, clothing, and shoes

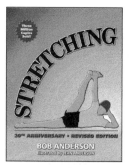

Stretching
20th Anniversary Revised Edition
by Bob Anderson

One of the world's most popular fitness books, now revised.

- 3½ million copies sold, in 23 languages
- Stretching routines for all sports (including running and everyday activities)
- New hand and wrist stretches for carpal tunnel problems

"A must-read for anyone who wants to stay supple for life."

–The Washington Post

Getting Stronger
2nd Edition
by Bill Pearl

A revised edition of the best-seller on weight training. Of special interest to runners are off-season and in-season weight training programs for distance running and new rehab exercises for knees.

- 550,000 copies sold
- 80 one-page training programs
- General conditioning, sports training, and bodybuilding

"A must for anyone serious about fitness."

–Newsday

Getting in Shape:
Workout Programs for Men and Women
by Bob Anderson, Bill Pearl, and Ed Burke

A unique workout book for anyone who wants to get back in shape.

- Stretching, weightlifting, and cardiovascular training
- 3-point programs

"An all-in-one book by masters from each corner of the fitness triangle."

–Dallas Morning News

More on Stretching
from Bob and Jean Anderson

Stretching Posters

Easy-to-read, 22½ × 34 inch and 17 × 22 inch wall posters are great visual aids for learning how to stretch. A total of 48 posters on 35 different sports, on body parts (lower back, neck/shoulder/arms, groin and hip, etc.), and miscellaneous subjects such as pregnancy, over 50, kids' stretches, partner stretches. Also a wall chart on computer and desk stretches that can be posted in the office. All posters available in laminated versions.

Stretching for Working America by Bob Anderson and Sally Carlson

Written for workers, people who work with their hands and bodies. Stretching before doing physical labor has been proven to reduce workplace injuries. The programs can be used by the individual worker or as part of an organized program for business, large or small.

Stretch and Strengthen by Bob Anderson and Dr. Donald G. Bornell

Individual stretching and strengthening exercises instruct people in wheelchairs, the disabled, and elderly. Also an excellent tool for rehabilitation. Comes with "Isoband" elastic exercise band for progressive resistance training to be done while sitting.

Stretching, The Video

A 57-minute video that is organized into comfortably paced sections. First there is an introduction to stretching. Then body parts, divided into neck and back, then legs and hips, followed by stretches for the feet and then arms and shoulders. Then there is a 14-minute program to use for everyday fitness or for specific sports and activities.

Body Tools

Excellent aids in helping reduce muscle tension and pain. All of these can be used in the office. *(See pp. 92 to 93.)*

To contact Stretching, Inc. *for a free 4-color catalog of these and other fitness products, write Stretching, Inc., P.O. Box 767, Palmer Lake, CO, 80133 or call 800-333-1307.*
Email: *office@stretching.com*   **Website:** *www.stretching.com*

Software That Reminds You to Stretch

StretchWare

by Bob Anderson

for Macintosh and Windows 95/98/ME/NT/2000/XP

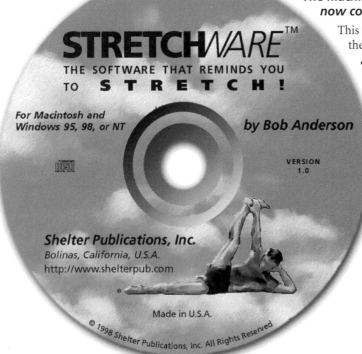

STRETCH*WARE*™

THE SOFTWARE THAT REMINDS YOU TO **S T R E T C H !**

For Macintosh and
Windows 95, 98, or NT

by Bob Anderson

VERSION
1.0

Shelter Publications, Inc.
Bolinas, California, U.S.A.
http://www.shelterpub.com

Made in U.S.A.

© 1998 Shelter Publications, Inc. All Rights Reserved

The machine that causes the problem now contains the solution!

This new computer program is based on the book, *Stretching in the Office.*

- Periodically, your computer asks if you want to stretch.
- If you say yes, the stretches appear on screen.
- When you roll your mouse over a stretch, instructions for that stretch pop up in a small window.
- You set your own preferences as to timing, types of stretches, sounds, etc.

"An electronic tap-on-the-shoulder."
—*San Jose Mercury News*

"A great program, ingeniously simple, yet highly effective. It works seamlessly with other software. . . ."
—*PA Today*

Test Drive StretchWare™!
Download a fully-functioning version that you can try out for 30 days.

www.stretchware.com

Shelter Publications
P. O. Box 279
Bolinas, CA 94924
415-868-0280
800-307-0131 (orders)